WORLD FOOTBALL

STEVE TONGUE

TREASURE PRESS

The sort of tackling which modern forwards have to put up with: Argentina's Diego Maradona is fouled by a Bulgarian defender during the 1986 World Cup finals, in which he established himself as the world's greatest player.

Art Editor
David Rowley

Designer
Simon Loxley

Editor
Andrew Jefford

Picture Research
Rona Skene

Production
Peter Thompson

First published in 1986 by
Treasure Press
59 Grosvenor Street
London WIX 9DA

© 1986 Octopus Books Limited

ISBN 1 85051 157 8

Printed in West Germany

CONTENTS

WORLD FOOTBALL

While England immodestly claims to have taught the rest of the world how to play football, its street games of the 13th and 14th centuries were almost certainly pre-dated by similar games in Ancient Greece and China.

No matter. By 1910, most of Europe and South America was playing, not just in the street and on waste ground but in full international matches watched by tens of thousands.

Now FIFA, the world governing body, boasts 150 member countries and the overall television audience for a World Cup final is estimated at two thousand million.

Football, the people's game, has become the world game.

Numbers indicate the ordering of countries in Chapter One.

EUROPEAN NATIONS

1 Republic of Ireland
2 Scotland
3 England
4 Northern Ireland
5 Wales
6 Belgium
7 France
8 Luxembourg
9 Spain
10 Portugal
11 Holland
12 West Germany
13 East Germany
14 Poland
15 USSR
16 Czechoslovakia
17 Austria
18 Switzerland
19 Italy

Bryan Robson, the England captain, whose unrelenting style has brought him numerous injuries over the course of his career. Shoulder dislocation took him out of the 1986 World Cup finals.

THE AMERICAS

1 Canada

2 USA

3 Mexico

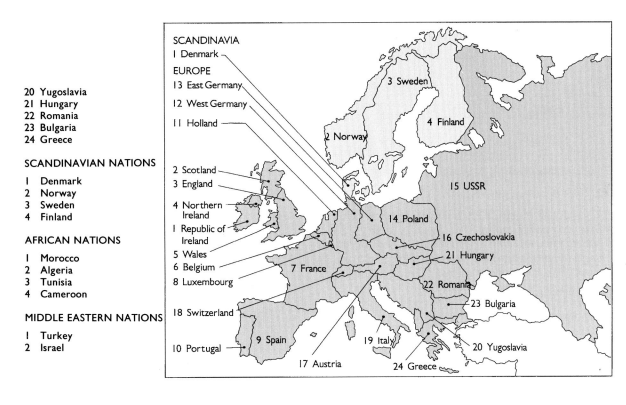

SCANDINAVIA
1 Denmark

EUROPE
13 East Germany
12 West Germany
11 Holland
2 Norway
3 Sweden
4 Finland
2 Scotland
3 England
4 Northern Ireland
1 Republic of Ireland
5 Wales
6 Belgium
8 Luxembourg
7 France
18 Switzerland
9 Spain
10 Portugal
17 Austria
19 Italy
14 Poland
16 Czechoslovakia
21 Hungary
22 Romania
23 Bulgaria
20 Yugoslavia
24 Greece
15 USSR

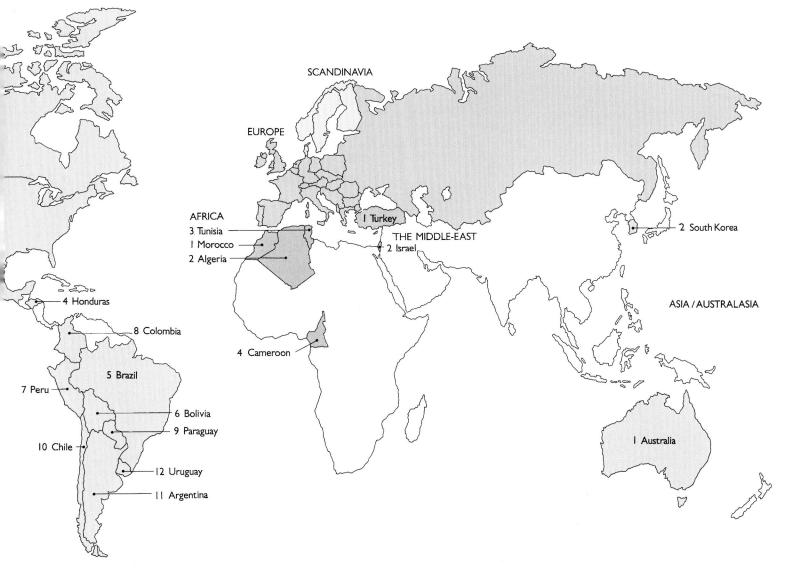

SCANDINAVIA

EUROPE

15 USSR

AFRICA
3 Tunisia
1 Morocco
2 Algeria

1 Turkey

THE MIDDLE-EAST
2 Israel

2 South Korea

4 Honduras

8 Colombia

4 Cameroon

ASIA / AUSTRALASIA

5 Brazil

7 Peru

6 Bolivia

9 Paraguay

10 Chile

12 Uruguay

11 Argentina

1 Australia

5

REPUBLIC OF IRELAND

*T*he history of football in the Republic of Ireland has been tortuous.

There was a split in 1921 with the North, which insisted on calling its team 'Ireland', a name only amended by FIFA in 1954. Until 1949 players often used to represent both Northern Ireland and the Republic. More recently those born in England of Irish descent have been eligible to play for the Republic.

Even this wider choice failed to bring anything like the success that might have been expected with players like Mark Lawrenson and Kevin Sheedy added to Liam Brady, Frank Stapleton and David O'Leary.

One oddity revived in 1985 was for a team from Northern Ireland (Derry City) to play in the Republic of Ireland's league, where the side's predominantly Catholic supporters feel much more at home.

FA formed: 1921 (all-Ireland FA formed 1880)
First international: 1924 v. Bulgaria 1–0 (Paris)
Most League titles: Shamrock Rovers

SCOTLAND

*S*cotland had the distinction of sharing in the first international soccer match, but has often seemed more interested in beating England than making an impression on a wider audience.

Losing only two of their first 33 internationals, the Scots played another 107 before deigning to meet opposition from outside Britain!

A 7–0 defeat by Uruguay when Scotland finally competed in the World Cup (1954) did not radically modify this attitude, though following the success of Glasgow Celtic and then Rangers in European competition the country became a regular World Cup finalist.

The 1986 campaign was marred by the death of manager Jock Stein just after a decisive tie in Wales. His successor Alex Ferguson was also in charge of Aberdeen

Battle of the midfielders: Scotland's Strachan (7) and Souness dispute possession with Brazil's Falcão (15) and Cerezo in a Group 6 match in the 1982 World Cup. Brazil won 4–1.

who, with Dundee United, had broken the 90-year dominance of Glasgow's two giants.

FA formed: 1873
First international: 1872 v. England 0–0 (Glasgow)
Honours: World Cup qualifiers 1954, 1958, 1974, 1978, 1982, 1986
European Youth winners 1982
European Cup winners Glasgow Celtic 1967; runners-up Glasgow Celtic 1970
European Cup Winners' Cup winners Glasgow Rangers 1972; Aberdeen 1983; runners-up Rangers 1961, 1967
Most League titles: Rangers

ENGLAND

England and West Germany in the 1966 World Cup final. Left to right: Uwe Seeler (German captain), Martin Peters, Bobby Moore (England captain), Nobby Stiles, and Bobby Charlton.

*E*ngland's acknowledged position as the home of football has been a weakness as well as a strength: it resulted early on in a most commendable missionary zeal, but later in a destructive arrogance and short-sighted insularity.

Refusal to enter the prewar World Cups led to delusions about the country's natural superiority persisting until two traumatic defeats by Hungary (6–3 and 7–1) in 1953–4.

There were poor showings in the postwar World Cups until the 1966 Wembley triumph, then a barren decade mitigated to some

extent by remarkable successes in the club competitions.

Sadly, England taught the world football hooliganism, too, and

reaped the rewards after the Brussels tragedy of May 1985.

FA formed: 1863
First international: 1872 v. Scotland 0–0 (Glasgow)
Honours: World Cup winners 1966; also qualified 1950, 1954, 1958, 1962, 1970, 1982, 1986
Olympic winners (as Great Britain) 1908, 1912
European Under-21 champions 1982, 1984
European Youth champions 1948, 1963, 1964, 1971, 1972, 1973, 1975, 1980; runners-up 1958, 1965, 1967
European Cup winners Manchester United 1968, Liverpool 1977, 1978, 1981, 1984, Nottingham Forest 1979, 1980, Aston Villa 1982; runners-up Leeds 1975,

Liverpool 1985
European Cup Winners' Cup winners Tottenham 1963, West Ham 1965, Manchester City 1970, Chelsea 1971, Everton 1985; runners-up Liverpool 1966, Leeds 1973, West Ham 1976, Arsenal 1980
Fairs'/UEFA Cup winners Leeds 1968, 1971, Newcastle 1969, Arsenal 1970, Tottenham 1972, 1984, Liverpool 1973, 1976, Ipswich 1981; runners-up London XI 1958, Birmingham City 1960, 1961, Leeds 1967, Tottenham 1974
'**Most League titles:** Liverpool

NORTHERN IRELAND

*P*olitical problems have dogged Irish football for decades: for whereas one team represents all-Ireland at Rugby Union, soccer has been split in two for more than 60 years, since 1921, and for more than three years in the 1970s no other country would visit Belfast. Yet at World Cup level Northern Ireland has a most commendable record, qualifying three times

against the odds.

From 1887 until 1957 the country had only ever played other British teams and France (twice). But the 1958 Northern Ireland side captained by Tottenham's Danny Blanchflower eliminated Portugal and Italy from the World Cup, and then reached the last eight before losing to France.

Billy Bingham, holder of 56 caps, took the

team to Spain in 1982 and Mexico in 1986. Sadly the country's finest player, George Best, never graced the finals.

FA (all-Ireland) formed: 1880
First international: 1882 (all-Ireland) v. England 0–13 (Belfast)
Honours: World Cup qualifiers 1958, 1982, 1986
European Youth runners-up 1963
Most League titles: Linfield

WALES

Not only do the best Welsh players gravitate towards the English Football League – the country's leading clubs do, too. Cardiff, Newport, Swansea and Wrexham have all played in it for many years but have also been able, by winning the Welsh Cup (in which some English teams also take part!) to compete in Europe. Cardiff City's run to the semifinal in 1968 is the best Welsh achievement there.

The national side, which had beaten England at home and away within six years of its formation, has more recently been involved in a series of dramatic failures to qualify for the World Cup and for the European Championship.

In 1975, 1977 and 1985 the Welshmen could point to a harsh penalty awarded to Yugoslavia, Scotland, and then Scotland again: they were eliminated in 1981 on goal difference and in 1983 by a last-minute goal. A team with Ian Rush and Mark Hughes in attack, and with Neville Southall and Kevin Ratcliffe in defence, would have been worth watching in Mexico.

So the high point so far remains a quarter-final place in the 1958 World Cup, when with John Charles out injured Wales lost only 1–0 to Brazil.

FA formed: 1876
First international: 1876 v. Scotland 0–4 (Glasgow)
Honours: World Cup qualifier 1958

BELGIUM

One of only four European countries to travel to Uruguay for the first World Cup in 1930, Belgium had by that time been playing international football for almost 30 years.

The Belgians had taken the Olympics gold medal in 1920, when their Czecho-slovak opponents walked off the field in protest at having a player dismissed. Holland has always been the most popular national opponent and in 1962 the 100th fixture between them was played.

Success at club level by the leading teams, notably Anderlecht, culminated in the national team reaching the 1980 European Championship final, losing 2–1 to West Germany.

Italian-born but qualifying for Belgium, Enzo Scifo is a brilliant midfielder for Anderlecht. Here (red strip) he takes on a couple of defenders in a match between Belgium and France.

FA formed: 1895
First international: 1904 v. France 3–3 (Brussels)
Honours: World Cup 4th 1986; also qualified 1930, 1934, 1938, 1954, 1978, 1982
European Championship runners-up 1980; 3rd 1972
European Youth champions 1977; runners-up 1952
Olympic winners 1920
European Cup runners-up Bruges 1976.
European Cup Winners' Cup winners Anderlecht 1976, 1978; runners-up Anderlecht 1977, Standard Liège 1982
Fairs'/UEFA Cup runners-up Anderlecht 1970, 1984 Bruges 1976
Most League titles: Anderlecht

FRANCE

Patrick Battiston (5), a regular choice for France's defence over the past few seasons, repels a Spanish attack in the 1984 European Championship final in Paris, where France won 2–0.

Despite having instigated almost all of European football's leading competitions, through the vision of men like Robert Guérin, Jules Rimet, Henri Delauney and Gabriel Hanot, there have been only two periods when France threatened to win them.

It was the mid-1950s before Reims suddenly flourished under its coach Albert Batteux, reaching two European Cup finals. Six of the club's players, plus Raymond Kopa (recently sold to Real Madrid), joined forces in a splendid national team that took 3rd place at the 1958 World Cup, Kopa linking up again to great effect with Just Fontaine, who scored a record 13 goals.

Batteux's talents later revived St-Etienne before the age of Michel Platini made soccer as well as rugby a source of national sporting pride again.

FA formed: 1919
First international: 1904 v. Belgium 3–3 (Brussels)
Honours: World Cup 3rd 1958, 1986; 4th 1982; also qualified 1930, 1934, 1938, 1954, 1966, 1978
European Championship winners 1984; semifinal 1960
Olympic winners 1984
European Youth champions 1949, 1983; runners-up 1950, 1968
European Cup runners-up Reims 1956, 1959, St-Etienne 1976
UEFA Cup runners-up Bastia 1978
Most League titles: St-Etienne

LUXEM-BOURG

Ranking among the smallest minnows of European football, Luxembourg remains an enthusiastic participant in all competitions.

A draw at the full international level, however, remains a source of very great celebration. Holding Iceland 0–0 in front of 500 people in 1985 ended a run of 32 straight defeats over a five-year period – although it still left Luxembourg seeking a first win since 1973!

One victory does stick out. Playing at home to Portugal in a 1961 World Cup qualifier, a hat trick by a locksmith called Andy Schmidt helped little Luxembourg win 4–2.

There has been a national league since 1910 with Jeunesse of Esch the most regular of the winners.

FA formed: 1908
First international: 1911 v. France 1–4 (Luxembourg)
Most League titles: Jeunesse Esch

SPAIN

Although Spain should be counted as one of the greatest footballing nations, its reputation rests largely on the achievement of two clubs, Real Madrid and Barcelona – above all Real, whose late-1950s team set the standards for all Europe.

While these two have remained formidable opponents in European competition and fierce rivals at home, the national side has repeatedly stumbled, never making an impression in the World Cup, even in the

days when foreigners like Alfredo Di Stéfano could be 'naturalized' and included.

Like Italy, however, Spain remains a magnet for top players and coaches from all over the world.

Spain's Lopez Alfaro (16) powers through an attempted trip by France's Fernandez in the 1984 European Championship final.

FA formed: 1905
First international: 1920 v. Denmark 1–0 (Brussels)
Honours: World Cup 4th 1950; also qualified 1934, 1962, 1966, 1978, 1982, 1986
European Championship winners 1964; runners-up 1984
European Youth champions 1952, 1954; runners-up 1957, 1964
World Youth runners-up 1985
Olympics 3rd 1920
European Cup winners Real Madrid 1956, 1957, 1958, 1959, 1960, 1966; runners-up Real Madrid 1962, 1964, 1981, Barcelona 1961, Atlético Madrid 1974, Barcelona 1986
European Cup Winners' Cup winners Atlético Madrid 1962, Barcelona 1979, 1982, Valencia 1980; runners-up Atlético Madrid 1963, 1986, Barcelona 1969, Real Madrid 1971, 1983
Fairs'/UEFA Cup winners Barcelona 1958, 1960, 1966, Valencia 1962, 1963, Real Zaragoza 1964, Real Madrid 1985, 1986; runners-up Barcelona 1962, Valencia 1964, Real Zaragoza 1966, Athletic Bilbao 1977
Most League titles: Real Madrid

PORTUGAL

A late starter in international terms, Portugal first came to be noticed through the exploits of its champion club Benfica in the European Cup.

The team, led by Mario Coluna, won the 1961 final against Barcelona, who had knocked out Real Madrid. In 1962 Benfica held on to the trophy against Real with the country's greatest player Eusebio now in the ranks. Three other finals were all lost, but Portugal's name had

been made and was held in even greater esteem after a 3rd place in the 1966 World Cup.

After that – nothing, until a European Championship semifinal in 1984 in which the Portuguese might well have beaten a tired French team. Then in 1986 Fernando Gomes' scoring feats took them to only their second World Cup finals.

The domestic championships have been dominated so completely by the big three, Benfica, Porto

and Sporting Lisbon, that one lone title (1946) to Belenenses is the only one to have escaped them.

FA formed: 1914
First international: 1921 v. Spain 1–2 (Madrid)
Honours: World Cup 3rd 1966; also qualified 1986
European Championship semifinalists 1984
European Youth champions 1961; runners-up 1971
European Cup winners Benfica 1961, 1962; runners-up Benfica 1963, 1965, 1968
European Cup Winners' Cup winners Sporting Lisbon 1964; runners-up FC Porto 1984
Fairs'/UEFA Cup runners-up Benfica 1983
Most League titles: Benfica

1

HOLLAND

*T*he 1970s was the golden decade of Dutch football and should have been marked by at least one World Cup win. Yet in the finals of 1974 and 1978 the more talented Dutch team was unable to hold off the West German and Argentinian sides.

In between times the 1976 European Championship eluded Holland, too, so the only trophies were won at club level by old rivals Feyenoord and Ajax Amsterdam who, following the appointment of Rinus Michels at Ajax in 1965, took ten successive League titles between them as well as four successive European Cups.

Failure to turn professional until 1954 hindered Holland's development before that date, and in the 1980s there has been a sad decline at both international and domestic level.

FA formed: 1889
First international: 1905 v. Belgium 4–1 (Antwerp)
Honours: World Cup runners-up 1974, 1978; also qualified 1934, 1938
Olympics 3rd 1908, 1912; 4th 1920, 1924
European Youth runners-up 1948, 1949, 1970
European Cup winners Feyenoord 1970, Ajax 1971, 1972 1973; runners-up Ajax 1969
UEFA Cup winners Feyenoord 1974, PSV Eindhoven 1978; runners-up Twente Enschede 1975, AZ Alkmaar 1981
Most League titles: Ajax

GERMANY

For post-1945 period *see* East Germany page 12; West Germany below.

FA formed: 1900
First international: 1908 v. Switzerland 3–5 (Basle)
Honours: World Cup 3rd 1934; also qualified 1938

WEST GERMANY

West Germany's Gerd Müller (white shirt), the deadliest striker in international football during the 1970s, takes on Holland's Johan Neeskens (10) in the 1974 World Cup final. West Germany won 2–1, Müller providing the winner.

*S*tatistically, Europe's outstanding football nation, with a World Cup record matched only by Brazil and more than 20 appearances in European club finals. The record is all the more remarkable in that following the Second World War no internationals were permitted until 1950; and that the West German national league (Bundesliga) did not come into existence until 1964.

By 1954 a World Cup had been won, in sensational fashion against Hungary, and a place in the last four at least has been regularly achieved since.

As with Holland, the 1970s proved to be the outstanding decade, with victories in every major competition by the national side and by clubs like Bayern Munich and Borussia

Mönchengladbach.
See also East Germany page 12; Germany above.

FA (all-Germany) formed: 1900
First international: 1950 v. Switzerland 1–0 (Stuttgart)
Honours: World Cup winners 1954, 1974; runners-up 1966, 1982, 1986; 3rd 1970; 4th 1958; also qualified 1962
European Championship winners 1972, 1980; runners-up 1976
Olympics 4th 1952
European Under-21 runners-up 1982
World Youth winners 1981
European Youth champions 1981; runners-up 1954, 1972
European Cup winners Bayern Munich (München) 1974, 1975, 1976, Hamburg 1983; runners-up Eintracht
Frankfurt 1960, Borussia Mönchengladbach 1977, Hamburg 1980, Bayern Munich 1982
European Cup Winners' Cup winners Borussia Dortmund 1966, Bayern Munich 1967, Hamburg 1977; runners-up TSV Munich 1965, Hamburg 1968, Fortuna Düsseldorf 1979
Fairs'/UEFA Cup winners Borussia Mönchengladbach 1975, 1979, Eintracht Frankfurt 1980; runners-up Borussia Mönchengladbach 1973, 1980, Hamburg 1982; Cologne (Köln) 1986
Most League titles: IFC Nuremberg (Nürnberg)

EAST GERMANY

After the partition of Germany in 1945 there were higher priorities than football. It was not until 1952 that the DDR played a full international, and not until 1955 that it won one.

Now, however, the East Germans play a full part in the European Championship, World Cup and Olympics. Teams at both club and international level, although never exciting, have become hard to beat.

In their only World Cup finals the East Germans achieved a famous victory over host country West Germany in Hamburg to win their group. The goal was scored by Jürgen Sparwasser, of the European Cup Winners' Cup winners Magdeburg, who with Joachim Streich has been the country's best-known player.

See also Germany page 11; West Germany page 11.

FA formed: 1948
First international: 1952 v. Poland 0–3 (Warsaw)
Honours: World Cup qualifiers 1974
Olympic winners 1976; runners-up 1980; 3rd 1964, 1972
European Youth champions 1965, 1970; runners-up 1969, 1973
European Cup Winners' Cup winners Magdeburg 1974; runners-up Carl Zeiss Jena 1981

POLAND

Although its clubs enjoy only moderate success, Poland has become the most consistently successful Eastern European country – at least when it really matters, in World Cups.

It was considered a sensation when Poland knocked out England in 1973. Yet the team that had won the previous year's Olympics went on to take 3rd place in the finals and repeat the achievement in 1982.

Happily it was the Polish attacking players who caught the eye: the elegant Kazimierz Deyna, who was later to play briefly in England; Grzegorz Lato, top scorer with seven goals in the 1974 tournament; Zbigniew Boniek, who moved to Juventus from Widzew Łódź.

As in France, the top provincial clubs have repeatedly outshone those from the capital, with Ruch Chorzów,

Zbigniew Boniek, Poland's most distinguished football export (Juventus, AS Roma), is a brilliant dribbler, with vivid acceleration and a tremendous right-foot shot. Here he is in action for Poland against France in the 1982 World Cup play-off for third place, which Poland won 3–2.

Górnik Zabrze and Widzew Łódź the most successful.

FA formed: 1919
First international: 1921 v. Hungary 0–1 (Budapest)
Honours: World Cup 3rd 1974, 1982; also qualified 1938, 1978, 1986
Olympic winners 1972; runners-up 1976; 4th 1936
European Cup Winners' Cup runners-up Górnik Zabrze 1970
Most League titles: Ruch Chorzów

USSR

Oleg Blokhin, Dynamo Kiev's lightning-fast goal-scoring winger, has been the USSR's most famous player since the mid-1970s. Here he leaves Mike Duxbury trailing in the England v. USSR match at Wembley in June 1984, when the Russians outplayed England and won 2–0.

Football started here in Tsarist days but the Russians' international record was a fragmented one until the 1950s, since which time they have generally proved difficult opponents. Winners of the Melbourne Olympics, 1956, they qualified for their first World Cup two years later and have been regular contestants ever since, frequently reaching the last eight.

The national team has nevertheless often seemed to lack imagination and colour. When a club side of thrilling invention like Dynamo Tbilisi did emerge, the USSR did not benefit as much as it should have done from the talents of

Aleksandr Chivadze, Vladimir Gutsayev and David Kipiani. But Dynamo Kiev were brilliant winners of the 1986 European Cup Winners' Cup.

FA formed: 1912
First international: 1924 v. Turkey 3–0 (Moscow)
Honours: World Cup 4th 1966; also qualified 1958, 1962, 1970, 1982, 1986
European Championship winners 1960; runners-up 1964, 1972
European Youth champions 1966 (joint), 1967, 1976, 1978, 1984
European Under-21 winners 1980
World Youth runners-up 1979
Olympic winners 1956; 3rd 1972, 1976, 1980
European Cup Winners' Cup winners Dynamo Kiev 1975, 1986, Dynamo Tbilisi 1981; runners-up Dynamo Moscow 1972
Most League titles: Dynamo Moscow

CZECHO-SLOVAKIA

Football came to Prague only shortly after Vienna and Budapest, when the country was part of the Hapsburg empire; and by the 1930s the now independent Czechoslovakia was a serious rival to her Central European neighbours.

Apart from England this was the only country to beat the Austrian *Wunderteam*, winning in Vienna a year before reaching the 1934 World Cup final.

The team of Ladislav Novák (75 caps) and Josef Masopust also reached the final in 1962 and then 14 years later there was a remarkable triumph at the European Championship in Belgrade, when Anton Ondruš, Antonín Panenka, Marian Masný and Zdeněk Nehoda were all outstanding players.

FA formed: 1906
First international: 1920 v. Yugoslavia 7–0 (Antwerp)
Honours: World Cup runners-up 1934, 1962; also qualified 1938, 1954, 1958, 1970, 1982
European Championship winners 1976
Olympic winners 1980; runners-up 1920, 1964
European Youth champions 1968; runners-up 1982, 1983
European Cup Winners' Cup winners Slovan Bratislava 1969
Most League titles: Sparta Prague

AUSTRIA

Austria's match against Hungary in 1902 was the first official international played outside Britain. Soon Austria had one of the strongest Continental teams under the inspiration of Hugo Meisl.

The coach he appointed, Englishman Jimmy Hogan, helped create the *Wunderteam* of the 1930s, beaten in the 1934 World Cup semifinal by the eventual winner Italy.

In 1954 3rd place was achieved even though the competition came a couple of years too late for another outstanding national team.

Hans Krankl starred in the side that reached the second stage of the World Cup finals in 1978 and 1982 despite the moribund state of domestic football.

Pezzey (red shirt) in action for Austria against West Germany in a 1978 World Cup Group A match, Austria winning more easily than the 3–2 score suggests.

FA formed: 1904
First international: 1902 v. Hungary 5–0 (Vienna)
Honours: World Cup 3rd place 1954, 4th 1934; also qualified 1958, 1978, 1982
Olympic runners-up 1936
European Youth champions 1957
European Cup Winners' Cup runners-up Austria/WAC 1978, Rapid Vienna 1985
Most League titles: Rapid Vienna

SWITZER-LAND

Noted mainly as the administrative home of European and World football, Switzerland is still a country whose national team can win or draw matches it is expected to lose.

Without qualifying themselves for recent World Cups, the Swiss beat England, Romania and Denmark, and held the USSR and Hungary – while three times failing to defeat lowly Norway.

An outstanding performer in this period was Claudio Sulser whose club, Grasshoppers, captured the original Swiss League championship as far back as 1898 and has been a regular Euro-pean competitor.

Young Boys of Berne (1959) and FC Zurich (1964 and 1977) were European Cup semifinalists.

FA formed: 1895
First international: 1905 v. France 0–1 (Paris)
Honours: World Cup qualifiers 1934, 1938, 1950, 1954, 1962, 1966
Olympic runners-up 1924
Most League titles: Grasshoppers

ITALY

One of the greatest of football nations, with an endemic passion for the game, yet one whose influence on tactics has been largely detrimental. *Catenaccio*, the ultra-defensive tactic pioneered by Helenio Herrera of Inter Milan in the 1960s, spread far beyond Italy, and even with many of the world's best midfield players and forwards imported into it, the Italian League is still renowned for low scoring.

Vittorio Pozzo, father of the game there, had a much more imaginative approach, fostered during the time he was in Britain. He led the national team through the glorious 1930s when it won two World Cups and lost only 7 out of 65 internationals.

By 1958 the Italians were failing to qualify for the finals and in

1966 they suffered the humiliation of defeat by North Korea. But in 1982 the *Azzurri*, as the Italian national team is called, survived a bad start and surprised a poor field with decisive victories over Brazil, Argentina, Poland and West Germany to regain their crown.

1982 World Cup final: the Italians Marco Tardelli (centre) and Antonio Cabrini (kneeling) celebrate after the final whistle. The Azzurri (Blues) outplayed West Germany, winning 3–1.

FA formed: 1898
First international: 1910 v. France 6–2 (Milan)
Honours: World Cup winners 1934, 1938, 1982; runners-up 1970; 4th 1978; also qualified 1950, 1954, 1962, 1966, 1974, 1986
European Championship winners 1968; 4th 1980
European Youth champions 1958, 1966 (joint); runners-up 1959
Olympic winners 1936; 3rd 1928; 4th 1960, 1984
European Cup winners AC Milan 1963, 1969, Inter Milan 1964, 1965, Juventus 1985; runners-up Fiorentina 1957, AC Milan 1958, Inter Milan 1967, 1972, Juventus 1973, 1983, AS Roma 1984
European Cup Winners' Cup winners Fiorentina 1961, AC Milan 1968, 1973, Juventus 1984; runners-up Fiorentina 1962, AC Milan 1974
Fairs'/UEFA Cup winners AS Roma 1961, Juventus 1977; runners-up Juventus 1965, 1971
Most League titles: Juventus

YUGOSLAVIA

*Y*ugoslav teams, while often appearing to possess the perfect combination of Slavonic flair and Western application, have perhaps not achieved as much as they should have done.

Winning the 1968 European Championship would have meant a new high: France (5–1) and England were beaten, but in the final, host country Italy scored a barely deserved equalizer

before winning the replay.

Eight years later the Yugoslavs had no luck again, losing to West Germany in the semi-final, then to Holland in the 3rd place match, both in extra time.

Yugoslav clubs quite frequently reach the quarter-finals of the European competitions, but only Dynamo Zagreb, in 1967, has managed to win one.

FA formed: 1919
First international: 1920 v. Czechoslovakia 0–7 (Antwerp)
Honours: World Cup 4th 1962; also qualified 1930, 1954, 1958, 1974, 1982
European Championship runners-up 1960, 1968; 4th 1976
European Under-21 winners 1978
European Youth champions 1951, 1979; runners-up 1953, 1962, 1974, 1978
Olympic winners 1960; runners-up 1948, 1952, 1956; 3rd 1984; 4th 1980
European Cup runners-up Partizan Belgrade 1966
Fairs'/UEFA Cup winners Dynamo Zagreb 1967; runners-up Dynamo Zagreb 1963, Red Star Belgrade 1979
Most League titles: Red Star Belgrade

HUNGARY

England keeper Merrick fingertips the ball around a post, while defenders Billy Wright (extreme left) and England's future manager Alf Ramsey (extreme right) watch apprehensively in the celebrated match against Hungary at Wembley in November 1953. The Hungarians, arguably the finest national side in football history, annihilated England 6–3.

Like Austria, the country's first and most regular opponents, the Hungarians were active very early in the 20th century. By far their most notable period, however, followed the Second World War, beginning with an impressive few years even before the truly wonderful run that brought only one defeat in 48 full internationals between May 1950 and February 1956. That loss, of course, was in the 1954 World Cup final when Puskás and friends lost a 2–0 lead to the West Germans in the teeming rain of Berne.

But the 1956 Hungarian uprising changed everything. There was a brief revival as gifted striker Florian Albert took his country to two World Cup quarter-finals and Ferencváros to a Fairs' Cup triumph (1965), but then there followed a long period of drought and self-doubt before becoming

regular qualifiers again.

FA formed: 1901
First international: 1902 v. Austria 0–5 (Vienna)
Honours: World Cup runners-up 1938, 1954; also qualified 1934, 1958, 1962, 1966, 1978, 1982, 1986
Olympic winners 1952, 1964, 1968; runners-up 1972; 3rd 1960
European Cup Winners' Cup runners-up MTK 1964, Ferencváros 1975
Fairs'/UEFA Cup winners Ferencváros 1965; runners-up Ferencváros 1968, Újpesti Dózsa 1969
Most League titles: Ferencváros

ROMANIA

The enthusiastic support of football fan King Carol prompted Romania to travel further than any other country taking part in the first World Cup in Uruguay. There the Romanians were knocked out by the hosts, and four years later beaten by eventual runners-up Czechoslovakia; then 1938 brought a disastrous defeat by Cuba.

Success since the Second World War has been almost non-existent: one victory in the European Youth championship could not be built upon, and there was particularly keen disappointment over unexpected failure to qualify for the 1982 and 1986 finals, when the damage was done by home defeats against Switzerland and Northern Ireland.

Most successful of the clubs – most of which were reorganized after the war – have been the two Bucharest teams Dinamo and Steaua, winners on penalties of the 1986 European Cup final against Barcelona.

FA formed: 1908
First international: 1922 v. Yugoslavia 2–1 (Belgrade)
Honours: World Cup qualifiers 1930, 1934, 1938, 1970
European Youth champions 1962; runners-up 1960
European Cup winners Steaua Bucharest 1986
Most League titles: Dinamo Bucharest

BULGARIA

The Bulgarian squad before a 1986 World Cup qualifying match against Luxembourg. Bulgaria has qualified five times for the finals of the tournament but has only once progressed beyond the first-round matches.

Students were the first enthusiastic devotees of the game in Bulgaria, where football in the early years was based on regions rather than clubs.

The first appreciable success, as the 1959 European Youth champions (the tournament was played in Sofia), was followed by qualification for the 1962 World Cup finals with an unexpected play-off victory over France.

The dominant team has been CSKA, the Bulgarian Army club that captured nine successive League titles from 1954 to 1962 (a European record at the time). After a riot during the Cup final against Levski Spartak Sofia in 1985 both clubs were disbanded and the League title awarded to Trakia Plovdiv.

The two clubs then effectively re-formed as Sredec and Vitosha respectively!

FA formed: 1923
First international: 1924 v. Austria 0–6 (Brussels)
Honours: World Cup qualifiers 1962, 1966, 1970, 1974, 1986
Olympic runners-up 1968; 3rd 1956
European Youth champions 1959, 1969
Most League titles: CSKA Sofia (formerly CDNA)

GREECE

Football in Greece has tended to be a turbulent affair, right from the days of the Intermediate Olympics in Athens in 1906, when military police were required in large numbers for the final after disturbances at the game between Athens and Salonika.

The 1920 Olympics in Belgium marked the international début of a scratch Greek team but, following a 9–0 defeat by Sweden, a national side did not play for another nine years!

Success since then has been isolated but all the more welcome for that – for example the 1980 European Championships in which, after qualifying by beating the USSR, the Greeks were able to hold the eventual winners West Germany 0–0, losing to Holland only 1–0 and Czechoslovakia, the holders, 3–1.

The Panathinaikos club, under Ferenc Puskás, unexpectedly reached the European Cup final at Wembley in 1971, losing to Ajax, then challenged Nacional of Uruguay for the World Club Championship.

FA formed: 1926
First international: 1920 v. Sweden 0–9 (Antwerp)
Honours: European Cup runners-up Panathinaikos 1971
Most League titles: Olympiakos

DENMARK

A crop of outstanding players emerging in the late 1970s suddenly made Denmark a force. Although all these men – Allan Simonsen, Frank Arnesen, Preben Elkjær-Larsen, Michael Laudrup, Morten Olsen and Jesper Olsen – moved abroad, just as their predecessors had done in the days before professionalism in 1978, they constituted a fine side when brought back for international duty.

Previous generations had also moved to the richer West German and Italian clubs, who descended with particular enthusiasm on the 1948 Olympics team.

Robbed of these players, however, Danish clubs have never been able to make any impression in European competitions. KB from Copenhagen, founded in 1876, is not only the leading club but also one of the oldest in the world.

Jesper Olsen, Manchester United's brilliant Danish winger, seen in action in Denmark's 4–2 victory against the USSR in the 1986 World Cup qualifying match at Copenhagen.

FA formed: 1889
First international: 1912 v. Norway 7–0 (Stockholm)
Honours: World Cup qualifiers 1986
European Championship semifinal 1984
Olympic runners-up 1908, 1912, 1960; 3rd 1948
Most League titles: KB Copenhagen

NORWAY

N orway remains poised one grade above the lowest-ranking countries of European soccer, and various developments over the last few years have suggested that it might well be able to improve its standing.

In 1981 Norway achieved a sensational World Cup victory over England in Oslo; then Yugoslavia was beaten 3–1 in the European Championship a year later. In 1985, too, the Norwegians won 2–1 away to the reigning world champions Italy.

The high point before that was a victory over Germany at the 1936 Berlin Olympics, this being followed by a win against Poland which gave Norway a proud 3rd place.

FA formed: 1902
First international: 1908 v. Sweden 3–11 (Gothenburg)
Honours: Olympics 3rd 1936
Most League titles: Fredrikstad

• 1 •

SWEDEN

Clearly Scandinavia's leading country until Denmark began to overshadow it in the 1980s, Sweden's record is a proud one for a nation of only eight million people.

The national championship is one of the oldest anywhere, first contested in 1896 when Örgryte won. Another Gothenburg club, IFK, soon emerged to challenge them, while Stockholm's AIK and Djurgården have remained leading clubs since the earliest days.

But it was Malmö FF, under the English coach Bob Houghton, who surprisingly reached the 1979 European Cup final. Three years later IFK won the UEFA Cup with an outstanding 3–0 second-leg victory over Hamburg.

The national team, Olympic champions in 1948, had its finest hour a decade later as World Cup hosts and runners-up.

Sweden's Nordqvist (centre) evades a Brazilian boot in a 1978 World Cup Group 3 match in Argentina. The game ended in a 1–1 draw.

FA formed: 1904
First international: 1908 v. Norway 11–3 (Gothenburg)
Honours: World Cup runners-up 1958; 4th 1938; also qualified 1934, 1974, 1978
Olympic winners 1948; 3rd 1924, 1952
European Cup runners-up Malmö 1979
Fairs'/UEFA Cup winners IFK Gothenburg 1982
Most League titles: Örgryte

FINLAND

With the same population as Denmark (around five million) but far fewer teams and no professionalism, Finland has never been able to achieve the same sort of break-through.

Apart from one solitary triumph in the Scandinavian Championships of 1963, honours have been counted in single matches rather than whole tournaments. A victory over Italy in the 1912 Olympics was the first of these; beating Northern Ireland and holding England in the 1984–5 season were more recent examples.

In 1986 Kuuysi Lahti became the first Finnish club to reach the European Cup quarter-final.

FA formed: 1907
First international: 1911 v. Sweden 2–5 (Helsinki)
Honours: Olympics 4th 1912
Most League titles: HJK Helsinki

MOROCCO ALGERIA

*M*orocco's appearance in the 1970 World Cup finals prepared the way for regular participation by other African countries. The Moroccans were the first team from that continent in the finals since Egypt in 1934, and were lucky to be there: they had beaten their keen 'local' rivals the Tunisians only on the toss of a coin. But what an impression they made! Only 8000 people turned up to see them play West Germany, beaten finalists four years earlier. But, amazingly, the jittery West Germans fell behind to a goal by Jarir Houmane, and only after two of Helmut Schön's typically astute substitutions did they equalize and then score a late winning goal.

Defeat by the very talented Peruvian side was no disgrace, and Morocco's first World Cup point followed with a deserved draw against Bulgaria.

Two years later Morocco reached the 1972 Olympics quarter-finals but missed out on further World Cups until 1986. There the team finished top of a group containing England, Poland and Portugal, before losing narrowly to eventual runners-up West Germany.

*Q*ualification for successive World Cups in 1982 and 1986 established Algeria's claims to be Africa's leading football power.

The Algerians made a fine impression in 1982 with a sensational victory over West Germany, followed by a win over Chile, and only the 'arranged' match between Austria and the Germans prevented them from reaching the second stage.

The goals against West Germany were scored by Algeria's outstanding player Lakhdar Belloumi, later to be voted African Sportsman of the Year, and Rabah Madjer, who joined the Portuguese club FC Porto.

The two leading clubs are JET, the African champions in 1981, and Mouloudia Chalia from Algiers. In the national championship three points are given for a win and two for a draw.

Algeria's striker Madjer (who has recently enjoyed a successful spell in Portugal with FC Porto), seen here in a 1982 World Cup Group 2 match against Austria, who won 2–0. A few days previously Algeria had caused the first sensation of the finals by beating West Germany 2–1.

1

TUNISIA

Tunisia's Temime (left) in a 1978 World Cup qualifying match against Egypt. Tunisia went through to the finals, where they drew with West Germany and beat Mexico in their Group 2 matches.

*T*unisia's football, like that of its great rival Morocco, was once under the jurisdiction of the French national federation.

After independence, the toss of a coin twice eliminated the Tunisians against the Moroccans in World Cup competitions, but then in 1977 a crowd of 120,000 in Tunis saw them defeat Egypt to qualify for the Argentina finals.

Putting behind them problems over a walk-out in an African Championship match against Nigeria, and political unrest at home, the Tunisians did extremely well. They defeated Mexico 3–1, but then lost rather unluckily 1–0 to Poland and, best of all, held the world champions West Germany 0–0.

Like Cameroon and Morocco, Tunisia was unable immediately to build upon this success, losing on penalties to Nigeria in the 1982

qualifying rounds, and being heavily beaten home and away by Algeria four years later.

CAMEROON

*C*ameroon, like Algeria, was desperately unlucky not to reach the second round of the World Cup finals on its début in 1982. The side drew each of its group matches, holding Italy 1–1 in the last of these when Cameroon had several good chances to win and eliminate the eventual victors.

Having joined FIFA in 1962, Cameroon has had considerable success in the various African competitions. Leading club Canon won the African Cup twice in three years (1978–80).

Inevitably the best players were snapped up by foreign clubs after 1982; goalkeeper Thomas N'Kono joined Español of Barcelona and Roger Milla went to Bastia and later St-Etienne.

TURKEY

Turkey's defender Yusuf shields the ball from England's captain Bryan Robson in the 1986 World Cup qualifier in Istanbul in November 1984. Turkey were routed 8–0, Robson scoring a hat trick.

Once professionalism was established in 1952, Turkey became an uncomfortable place for many distinguished visitors. In 1954 Spain lost there in the World Cup and it was in Istanbul that for the great Hungarian team an 18-match unbeaten run came to an end.

With West Germany held to a draw in 1979 and Austria beaten four years later (both in competitive games) it was a disappointment that only one point was gained from the 1986 qualifying group against England, Northern Ireland, Romania and Finland.

Fenerbahçe and Galatasary have been the principal clubs since football, previously declared illegal by the government, was legalized early this century, although Trabzonspor and Beşiktaş have also been seen in the European Cup.

ISRAEL

The Israelis have become increasingly isolated in world football, with neither Europe nor Asia wanting them. Their World Cup history is littered with teams refusing to play them.

Although they appeared to have found a home in Asian football, they were placed in a European group for the 1966 World Cup, then put with New Zealand and Australia in 1970. The latter two proved easier opponents and paved the way for Israel's first appearance in the finals.

Building on the experience gained in the 1968 Olympics in Mexico, Israel drew with Sweden and then the eventual runners-up Italy.

Expelled from the Asian federation, the Israelis were back in Europe for 1982, then Oceania for 1986, losing this time to both Australia and New Zealand.

AUSTRALIA

Australia's Charlie Yankos is beaten by Scotland's Frank McAvennie in the 1986 World Cup play-off between the winners of the Oceania Group and the Group 7 runners-up. Australia lost this first leg 0–2 in Glasgow, drawing the second leg 0–0.

Soccer in Australia, although more than 100 years old, has always been dogged by two principal problems: vast distances between the big cities, and the much greater popularity of various forms of rugby.

Success in reaching the 1974 World Cup finals brought enough interest to prompt the formation of a national championship, but it lasted only from 1977 to 1983; Sydney City Hakoah won the title four times.

A series of coaches, German, British and Yugoslav, came and went trying to build on the achievement of 1974. Frank Arok led the national team through the 1986 qualifying rounds, when the Australians put up two vigorous displays before losing the play-off against Scotland.

SOUTH KOREA

South Korea's appearance in the 1986 World Cup finals helped even the score with communist North Korea, whose team is still remembered with great affection for its quite astonishing performances against the Italian and Portuguese teams in 1966.

South Korea had reached the 1954 finals and been heavily beaten not only by Hungary but by Turkey as well. South Korea remains one of Asia's strongest footballing countries, having turned professional some years ago when a national league was established.

Cha Boom Kun, the outstanding player, was picked up by Eintracht Frankfurt, later moving on to another West German club, Bayer Leverkusen.

CANADA

Canada's squad for the 1986 World Cup. Surprising qualifiers, the Canadians gave a good account of themselves in Mexico against the formidable USSR, France and Hungary sides.

As in Australia, loyalties to Canadian clubs are largely ethnic, but domestic football has picked up the pieces left by the 1985 demise of the North American Soccer League, in which Toronto Blizzard and Vancouver Whitecaps had both been a force.

When the best players from the various immigrant groups were pulled together, Canada reached the Olympics quarter-finals in 1984, only losing to Brazil on a penalty shoot-out. Then with much the same team the Canadians beat Haiti, Guatemala, Costa Rica and Honduras to reach the 1986 World Cup finals in Mexico.

USA

Two severe blows in the space of two years threatened the future prospects of soccer in the United States. First, in 1983, FIFA ignored the country's claims to take over the World Cup finals from Colombia, denying the Americans an opportunity that would have produced massive publicity and equally big crowds. Then the North American Soccer League folded after 17 years. The events were not unconnected. The only reasons for optimism now are continued reports of keenness in schools and colleges, and the comparative success of indoor soccer.

The Americans' greatest achievement in soccer was back in 1950 when they beat England 1–0 in the World Cup – one of the most unexpected results in football history.

1

MEXICO

*M*exico has benefited more than any other country from its geographical position – not only playing at altitude, but also being surrounded by a cluster of rivals unable to provide much opposition in World Cup qualifiers.

In tournament after tournament powerful European nations have looked on enviously as Mexico claimed a qualifying place yet again. The Mexicans' record in recent finals, apart from the two they have staged, is all too revealing: played 20, won 1, drawn 3, lost 16; the sole victory came in 1962 against Czecho-slovakia, who had already qualified for the quarter-finals.

Two World Cups have at least left the country with some fine stadia, above all the Azteca in Mexico City with its 110,000 capacity, shared by the leading Mexican clubs America and Necaxa.

Mexico's Xavier Aguirre (13) congratulated by his team mates after scoring against Italy in June 1985. The match was part of a friendly mini-tournament held at Mexico City's Azteca stadium, England and West Germany also taking part.

HONDURAS

*T*his will always be remembered as the country that lost a World Cup tie which started a war. In the 1969 qualifying competition Honduras lost a play-off to neighbour and old enemy El Salvador in neutral Mexico City. Violence followed along the border for several days and an estimated 3000 died.

Relations and matches between the two countries have been even more tense ever since. In 1982 they again had to meet three times; the Hondurans squeezed through to Spain, where they were one of several supposed minnows who almost swallowed some bigger fish – they drew with the host country and with the group winner Northern Ireland.

Four years later the Honduran team again knocked out El Salvador, but then suffered unexpected difficulties against Canada.

BRAZIL

Brazil's Zico in action against Italy in the 1982 World Cup – a thrilling match unexpectedly won 3–2 by the Italians. Zico, possibly the world's greatest player during the early 1980s, combines great tactical cunning with a mastery of the killing pass, a ferocious shot with either foot, and an intimidating repertoire of dead-ball ploys.

The most naturally gifted football nation in the world, which has nevertheless had mixed results trying to match those talents to European determination and tenacity.

In the early years Brazil was frequently outstripped by Uruguay and Argentina, and achieved international prominence only after turning professional and taking 3rd place in the World Cup in 1938. Beaten when hosts and hot favourites in 1950, the Brazilians' first great success was eight years later when Pelé was thrust into the team that won the World Cup in Sweden, and then retained it in Chile.

Brazil's great 1970 victory was an exultant one, but for most observers the European influence since then has been a negative factor.

Club football, from the Copacabana beach matches to the World Club championship, is dominated by the teams of Rio de Janeiro (Flamengo and Fluminese) and São Paulo (Santos and Corinthians – whose name recalls the British influence on the earliest days of football in Brazil).

BOLIVIA

Such distinction as Bolivia has achieved has been almost entirely due to the advantage of playing home matches 3660 m (12,000 ft) above sea level. It was there that the country won the South American Championship in 1963, when world champions Brazil among others fielded a much-weakened side.

Rare triumphs for the Bolivians outside their own country include a 1–1 draw in Rio de Janeiro in a qualifying match for the 1986 World Cup. In two tournaments in which they reached the finals (1930 and 1950) they totalled only three matches, losing 4–0, 4–0 and 8–0.

Of the Bolivian clubs, The Strongest is also the oldest – it won the first national championship in 1914 and has taken more titles than any other.

PERU

Peru's José Velasquez in action in the 1982 World Cup Group I match against Cameroon (green strip). A country often throwing up brilliant individual talents, Peru reached the World Cup finals in 1930, 1970, 1978, and 1982.

H istorically the best of the 'second grade' of South American countries behind the big three Argentina, Brazil and Uruguay, Peru was the first nation to break their domination of the South American Championship by winning the 1939 title in the Peruvian capital Lima.

In 1975 the Peruvians won again on a play-off against Colombia.

There were also two outstanding World Cups. In 1970 Peru eliminated Argentina, and then proved to be one of the most exciting teams in the finals, coached by the former Brazilian star Didí (Walter Pereira): his 4–2–4 formation produced 16 goals in four matches, and a quarter-final defeat by Brazil was entirely honourable.

Eight years later Peru won a group including Holland and Scotland, only to be outplayed in the second round. But

defeat by Chile in the 1986 qualifying rounds was a jolt.

COLOMBIA

C olombia's greatest contribution to world football should have been the staging of the 1986 World Cup finals, but fears about the size of the competition and the magnitude of the task led to a reluctant withdrawal in 1982. Instead the country is best known for the 'pirate' league set up outside the jurisdiction

of FIFA in 1950, which snatched stars as brilliant as Alfredo Di Stéfano without paying transfer fees.

For Colombia to qualify for the World Cup finals tends to require a particularly weak group. It has been managed only once, in 1962, when holding the USSR 4–4 was a stunning result. In the 1986 competition

Colombia lost only two of the initial six group matches, but was beaten in a play-off with Paraguay.

Deportivo Cali, which rivals Millionarios and Independiente as leading club, once got as far as the South American Club final (1978), but lost to Boca of Argentina.

PARAGUAY

Paraguay's squad that drew with Chile 2–2 in November 1985 in course of qualifying for the 1986 World Cup. The side depends heavily on the flair of Julio César Romero (universally known as Romerito), one of the most gifted players in South America.

Paraguay is another country with a number of proud achievements despite the handicap of acute poverty. Foremost among these was a remarkable treble in 1979–80 when the national side won the South American Championships by beating Brazil in the semifinal and Chile in the final. Then Olimpia, Paraguay's dominant club, won first the South American Cup and later the World Clubs' Cup.

Olimpia was coached by former Uruguayan international Luis Cubilla, who returned in 1985 after spells with two of South America's top clubs, Peñarol and River Plate.

Paraguay competed in the first World Cup and also in the finals of 1950, 1958 (losing 7–3 to France but beating Scotland) and 1986.

CHILE

Third place in the 'home' World Cup of 1962 must seem a very long time ago to the Chilean football enthusiasts, most of whose clubs are now facing severe financial difficulties. It was by no means an outstanding team in 1962, yet one good enough to beat Italy in the notorious 'Battle of Santiago', then the USSR in the quarter-final and Yugoslavia in the 3rd place play-off.

Since then, curiously, Chile has qualified only for the finals held in Europe, managing just six goals and no victories in nine games.

A national club championship has been staged since 1933 with Colo Colo (named after a legendary Indian hero) the most successful side. Cobreola has twice reached the South American Club final, taking Flamengo of Brazil to a play-off in 1981.

ARGENTINA

Diego Maradona, the chunky, immensely strong genius of Argentinian soccer. A mesmerizing dribbler, who can bend the ball with shots from either foot, his appetite for goals is undimmed in spite of grievous injuries inflicted by ruthless defences in the Spanish and Italian leagues.

Argentina has always shared Brazil's fanaticism for football without finding such joyous expression for it, and in the past 30 years has suffered violent outbursts both on and off the field. The death of one spectator in 1985 brought a two-week suspension of the national league.

On the field the mid-1960s was a depressing period for footballing relations with other countries, culminating in wild scenes when Racing Club and Estudiantes met Glasgow Celtic, Manchester United, Milan and Feyenoord for the World Clubs Cup.

Possibly because of this clouded reputation, Argentina's 1978 World Cup win was greeted with muted acclaim elsewhere. It could not prevent a continued exodus of top players to financially more stable countries. But victory in 1986 on the back of Maradona's brilliance was more generously received.

URUGUAY

Although organized football started earlier in Argentina, and Brazil has earned a greater reputation, Uruguay's achievements, for such a small country, match those of its rivals in many ways.

For a long period Uruguay outstripped the others, winning five out of the first eight South American Championships (1916–26); successive Olympics tournaments (1924 and 1928); then two of the first four World Cups (1930 and 1950).

Even later, when a South American Clubs Cup began, Peñarol from Montevideo was victorious in the first two seasons.

However, 4th places in the World Cups of 1954 and 1970 were interspersed with and followed by some rather disappointing performances.

AJAX AMSTERDAM

*A*lthough this remains Holland's best-known club, Ajax's achievements outside its home country are confined to a period of only five years. Between 1969 and 1973 the team constructed by Rinus Michels, and topped off by Stefan Kovacs, reached four European Cup finals, winning the last three in succession. Equally important was the freewheeling style of a side packed with accomplished foot-ballers who could fill any position on the field at any given time.

Four players appeared in each of those finals: the majestic Johan Cruyff, Piet Keizer, Wim Suurbier and Barry Hulshoff. A little younger, but present for the hat trick of wins, were goalkeeper

Heinz Stuy, Johan Neeskens, Gerrie Muhren, Arie Haan and the German Horst Blankenburg.

For the 1973 victory over Juventus another talented youngster, Johnny Rep, came in on the left wing and scored the only goal.

Ajax showed no enthusiasm for the traditional World Clubs Cup match against South America's champions. In 1971 the Dutchmen were happy for the team they beat in the European Cup final that year, Panathinaikos, to compete in their place; and the following year's violent clashes with Independiente of Argentina only confirmed this mistrust. Then in 1973 Ajax set a precedent by playing

Cup Winners' Cup holders Glasgow Rangers instead: thus was the European Super Cup born.

Yet it all fell apart for Ajax almost as quickly as it had begun. In the summer of 1973 Cruyff followed Michels to Barcelona, Ajax lost its very first European Cup tie without him (to CSKA Sofia), and within a couple of years Neeskens, Rep, Muhren and Haan had gone abroad too.

Not until 1977 could Ajax even win the Dutch League or Cup again. Finding good young players scarce in Holland, the club put its faith in a series of Danes – Søren Lerby, Frank Arnesen, Jan Mølby and Jesper Olsen among them – instead.

The club was founded

in 1900 and won its first national title in 1918. Enjoying a run of five championships in nine years in the 1930s represented Ajax's zenith – until the golden 1970s.

Johan Cruyff, the greatest European player of the 1970s, inspired Ajax Amsterdam to a hat trick of European Cup triumphs in 1971–3. After playing later for Barcelona, then in the United States, and finally Feyenoord (who he led to the League and Cup double), he returned to Ajax as manager.

BAYERN MUNICH

The club now generally recognized as West Germany's biggest did not qualify for a place when a national league was first established as late as 1963. Bayern had to fight through the play-offs to reach the Bundesliga for its third season, but the men from Munich made an immediate impression by winning the Cup in their first year, the European Cup Winners' Cup in their second, and the Bundesliga in their third.

Having won the League again in 1972 the club moved from the humble Grünwald ground into the magnificent new Olympic stadium, completing a hat trick of League successes two years later as a hat trick of European Cups began.

That 1973–4 European campaign proved to be an eventful one. Åtvidaberg of Sweden was only beaten on penalties, Dynamo Dresden by 7–6 (4–3 3–3) and Atlético only in a replay earned by Georg Schwarzenbeck's last-minute goal.

The finals against against Leeds (2–0) and St-Etienne (1–0) did not see Bayern at its best, but with players like Franz Beckenbauer, Gerd Müller, Paul Breitner, Uli Hoeness and Sepp Maier the side had clearly succeeded Ajax as Europe's outstanding club.

When Müller left for Florida after scoring 365 Bundesliga goals, Karl-Heinz Rummenigge was able to take up a more central role in attack, helping the team to League titles in 1980 and 1981, and in the unsuccessful 1982 European Cup final against Aston Villa.

By 1985 the stars were Karl-Heinz's brother Michael and Dieter Hoeness, the brother of Uli who had become the club's general manager.

Bayern Munich's team celebrate after beating Leeds United 2–0 in the 1975 European Cup final in Paris — the second of their three consecutive victories. The tough, talented but tactically naïve English champions were beaten by a team of brilliant counter-punchers.

BENFICA

*T*he greatest of the three Portuguese clubs who dominate their country's football, having won more League titles than Sporting Lisbon and Porto put together since the initial championship of 1935. Like many other famous clubs, however, the current team is rather burdened by comparisons with its predecessors – notably the side that reached three successive European Cup finals to put Portuguese football on the map in the early 1960s.

If Eusebio is the single figure best remembered from that triumphant period, Hungarian coach Bela Guttmann was in fact the inspiration: a man who seemed to possess the Midas touch that all club chairmen and all presidents seek. Újpesti, AC Milan, São Paulo and Porto all benefited from it before Benfica got hold of him in the summer of 1959.

Drastically revising the playing staff, he brought in players like Germano, José Augusto, Joachim Santana, José Aguas and the captain Mario Coluna. The Portuguese championship duly followed and 12 months later victory, somewhat unexpectedly, against Barcelona in the first European Cup final played without Real Madrid.

Eusebio, bought like Coluna from the colony of Mozambique, scored twice in the dramatic 1962 final, a 5–3 triumph over the ageing Real side. Guttmann then left for Peñarol and Benfica was defeated in three subsequent European Cup finals.

Although the club ended its policy of not signing up foreigners in the late 1970s, it was another Portuguese player, Fernando Chalana, who starred in the 1983 Benfica team, narrowly beaten by Anderlecht in the UEFA Cup final.

Benfica's team that beat the supposedly invincible Real Madrid 5–3 in the thrilling and skilful European Cup final of 1962 in Amsterdam. The peerless Eusebio (second from left in the front row) scored two of Benfica's goals with pulverizing right-foot shots.

INTER MILAN

Irishman Liam Brady (blue stripes), once of Arsenal, plays for Internazionale after a spell with Sampdoria of Genoa. A brilliant, if essentially one-footed, midfielder, he helps make the bullets for Karl-Heinz Rummenigge, Inter's other import, to fire.

Founded in 1908 by a rebel group that had broken away from AC Milan, Inter nevertheless shares the Giuseppe Meazza stadium in San Siro with the great rival club. Inter's blue-and-black stripes counterpoint Milan's red-and-black.

Meazza was a star of the 1930s Inter and Italy teams in a period when Inter, Juventus and Bologna were the most successful clubs.

Inter's championship wins of 1953 and 1954 came just too soon for European competition and it was the mid-1960s before the club made an impact under Helenio Herrera, the itinerant Argentine coach. Luis Suarez came from Spain, winger Jair from Brazil (displacing Englishman Gerry Hitchens). Behind these talented forwards and Italian Sandro Mazzola, Herrera built a formidable defensive unit which nevertheless had a unique attacking weapon in left-back Giacinto Facchetti.

In its first European Cup season, 1963–4, Inter knocked out the champions of England (Everton), France (AS Monaco), Yugoslavia and West Germany, then beat Real Madrid, Puskás, Di Stéfano and all, in the final. A 1–0 win over Benfica the following year was altogether grimmer, as were the World Clubs Cup victories over Independiente.

Few tears were shed elsewhere when Glasgow Celtic, with attack as the club's watchword, defeated Herrera's men in the 1967 final and he had moved on by 1972 when they took revenge by beating the Scots on penalties after two goalless draws in the semifinal – and lost the final 2–0 to Ajax.

Inter has remained one of Italy's leading clubs, able to pay such transfer fees as the £3 million that bought Karl-Heinz Rummenigge, but without managing to land another European trophy.

JUVENTUS

Michael Laudrup (stripes, centre foreground), the devastatingly fast Danish striker, was for some time loaned by Juventus to Lazio of Rome. But he returned to Turin for the 1985–6 season to replace the Polish star Zbigniew Boniek, who was transferred to AS Roma.

Far and away Italy's most successful club in terms of League titles won, 'Juve' had to wait until 1985 to win the European Cup: when, of course, the whole event was overshadowed by the tragedy of 39 deaths, almost all of them Italian.

Twice, successful Italian World Cup teams had been built around the club's players – in 1934 Juventus supplied five players and in 1982 six, including on both these occasions the goalkeeper-captains, Giampiero Combi and Dino Zoff respectively. Combi's team won a

record five successive Italian titles (1931–5), a feat that Torino, co-tenants of the Stadio Communale, might have matched but for the Superga air disaster of 1949, which wiped out the whole team. Instead Juventus again led Turin's challenge to the Milanese clubs as millions of lire were spent bringing top foreign players to Italy in the 1950s.

Juventus took John and Karl Hansen from Denmark's 1948 Olympics team, then John Charles, 'the Gentle Giant' from Wales and Omar Sivori from Argentina for a world record £95,000.

Giampiero Boniperti, later to become club president, was captain of the side that won the Italian League in 1958 but had little luck in Europe. Even when five more titles were won in seven years during the 1970s the European Cup still proved elusive for the team of Zoff, Franco Causio and Roberto Bettega, who lost the 1973 final to Ajax.

In fact it took the introduction of a new wave of foreigners – above all Michel Platini – to restore the club as a force in Europe. With the Pole Zbigniew Boniek alongside him Juventus lost another European Cup final (to

Hamburg) but won the Cup Winners' Cup the following year, and in 1985 defeated Liverpool amid the carnage of Brussels.

LIVERPOOL

Frequently touted over the past ten years as the world's best club side, Liverpool has yet to win the competition that in theory decides that title. After winning its first European Cup finals (1977 and 1978) Liverpool declined to play against the South American champions. Then when the club fell for the lure of the yen and agreed to meet Flamengo of Brazil in Tokyo, Zico's team won 3–0.

It is undeniable, however, that from 1976 to 1986 the club dominated English football to a degree that few would ever have believed possible in this most competitive of countries.

The late Bill Shankly restored a club which, when he arrived as manager in 1959, had been in the Second Division for five years. Persuading (reluctant) directors that money had to be spent on players and facilities, he bought shrewdly enough to fashion a team that won the First Division championship at its second attempt (1964) and had an immediate impact in the European Cup, losing somewhat unluckily to Inter in the 1965 semifinal, and to Borussia Dortmund in the 1966 Cup Winners' Cup final.

Shankly's 'second' team, with Clemence, Hughes and Keegan (61, 62 and 63 England caps

respectively), won the League and UEFA Cup in 1973, and the FA Cup in 1974 – whereupon he staggered everyone by retiring. Although hurt by Liverpool's treatment of him thereafter, he was grateful that the club took his advice to promote all the staff he left behind. So Bob Paisley took over for a nine-year period of spectacular success. At home there were six championships, four League/Milk Cup wins in succession, another UEFA Cup and, most cherished, the European Cups of 1977, 1978 and 1981.

Another elder statesman, Joe Fagan, was then promoted as Paisley moved over for

two years, returning to help player-manager Kenny Dalglish, who took over in the aftermath of Brussels and astonishingly won the League and FA Cup double in his first season.

Liverpool's left-back Jim Beglin (in cap) and captain Alan Hansen parade around Wembley stadium after beating Everton in the 1986 FA Cup final. That afternoon Kenny Dalglish (extreme right) crowned his first astonishing season as player-manager by leading Liverpool to the League and Cup double.

MANCHESTER UNITED

A club that has only won one European trophy; once went 41 years without winning a domestic League title and has struggled for two decades to win another one – yet remains one of the most famous names in football. That is the paradox of Manchester United.

It would be quite untrue to say that the reputation is based purely on emotion born of the 1958 Munich air disaster, for the team was already established as the most powerful in England, returning as it was from Belgrade after ensuring itself a place in the last four of the European Cup.

Of the eight players who died, three were regular England internationals: Roger Byrne, Duncan Edwards and Tommy Taylor. The manager Matt Busby, already a much-loved figure, had to fight against the knowledge of those deaths as well as his own dreadful injuries. He survived and a full ten years later, when United beat Benfica to win the European Cup at last, it was Matt's night – for all the genius of George Best, the two goals of Bobby Charlton (another immensely popular Munich survivor) and the dramatic save by goalkeeper Alex Stepney from Eusebio which kept Manchester level.

Busby had taken over in February 1945, when United had not won the League since 1911, and had in fact been relegated three times. He took United to second place four times in five seasons, then the championship in 1952, before building his 'Busby Babes'.

When relegation threatened again in 1962, Denis Law (£115,000 from Torino) and Pat Crerand (£56,000 from Glasgow Celtic) were bought, laying the foundations for that eventual European Cup win (a match Law missed through injury).

Ron Atkinson was only continuing a tradition of big spending when he paid his former club West Bromwich Albion £1.5 million for Bryan Robson in 1981. Like Busby's immediate successors, he found further championships elusive as Liverpool and then Everton dominated the English game, but without winning hearts quite like Manchester United.

United's 1968 squad, with their manager, the great Matt Busby, pose with the European Cup, which they had won 4–1 in extra time in a pulsating final against Benfica at Wembley. Denis Law, who missed the match through injury, is third from left in the front row.

REAL MADRID

Real Madrid (seen here is the side for a 1979 cup match with Valencia) were the great champions of the early years of the European Cup, playing a quality of football which has rarely been equalled since at club or national level. They have played in no less than 13 finals of European club competitions.

If there was ever a greater club side than Real Madrid in the late 1950s, it is difficult to imagine where or when. Around the perfect footballer, Alfredo Di Stéfano, was built a cosmopolitan team whose rise coincided beautifully with the start of the European Cup and all the competitions that followed in its wake.

The foundations were laid much earlier, when Santiago Bernabeu, a former centre-forward, coach and secretary to Real, was appointed President. At that time the club had won only two of the first twelve Spanish League championships and played in a tatty stadium that held barely 15,000 people. Bernabeu immediately organized a

hugely successful share issue which paid for a new 75,000 capacity ground, adding another tier later with room for 50,000 more. As for building a team to go with it, the key was the signing in 1953 of Di Stéfano for £30,000.

He scored 27 goals in 30 games as Real won the 1954 title – its first for 21 years – and 26 the next season as the club retained it and became obvious candidates for the first European Cup.

Aside from the well-known statistics of Real's five successive triumphs, it is worth recalling that there were difficult games and even defeats. Milan beat the Madrid side 2–1 in the inaugural semifinal and in the subsequent epic final against Reims,

which made the competition, Real was 2–0 and then 3–2 down. Two years later Milan took Real to extra time in the final. Then in 1959, with Puskás now partnering Di Stéfano, the club needed a play-off to beat the local rival side Atlético.

However, 1960 brought one of the high points of football history: Real's glorious 7–3 win over Eintracht (making 31 goals in seven European Cup games that season).

Even when Barcelona knocked Real out in 1961, its domination of domestic football continued with eight titles in nine years. Real Madrid won the European Cup again in 1966, with left-winger Francisco Gento now captain, and it was not

until the 1970s that European success began to elude this great club.

AC MILAN

AC Milan has waged a long struggle with Internazionale and emerged with almost as many honours. Yet another club whose name betrays British origins, Milan became prominent soon after starting up in 1899, interrupting Genoa's run of six successive Italian championships by winning in 1901. However, following further successes in 1906 and 1907, and then the split with Inter a year later, Milan spent almost half a century trying to break the domination of the Turin clubs.

It took the inspired signing of three forwards from Sweden, Gunnar Gren, Gunnar Nordahl and Nils Liedholm, to win the 1951 championship (with 101 goals!), and the £72,000 spent on Uruguayan Juan Schiaffino in 1954 led to another title win and entry to the first European Cup.

Real Madrid beat Milan in the semifinal that first season and in the final of 1958, after Milan had twice been ahead. But by 1963 Real was out of the way and AC Milan surprised its successors Benfica by winning the Wembley final 2–1, the team inspired by midfielder Gianni Rivera having scored 33 goals in nine ties.

A more defensively orientated team counterattacked skilfully to win the Cup Winners' Cup in 1968, and the European Cup against a young Ajax a year later. But a betting scandal consigned Milan to the *Serie B* for the first time and in 1986 financial rescue was required to prevent bankruptcy.

ANDERLECHT

Anderlecht are Belgium's most successful side at international level. Anderlecht's De Groote tangles with Spurs' Danny Thomas in the second leg of the 1984 UEFA Cup final, won by Spurs on penalties.

The Belgian championship had been in existence for 12 years before the RSC Anderlechtois (to use the French form) was founded in 1908 – and not until 1947 did it win it! But there followed a notable period of success with 14 titles in 22 years, including five in succession between 1964 and 1968.

English coach Bill Gormlie was the inspiration in the late 1940s, while on the field the club's outstanding performers were the centre-forward Jef Hermans and, later, Jef Jurion in midfield and Paul Van Himst, winner of 81 Belgian caps, up front.

Still made up of only part-time professional players, Anderlecht was outclassed in the European Cup, conceding 10 goals to Nándor Hidegkuti's Red Banner in the first two-leg tie and losing 10–0 away to Manchester United a year later.

However, the 1970s erased those memories with a Fairs' Cup final appearance in 1970 (losing to Arsenal) followed by three more in the Cup Winners' Cup. West Ham was beaten in 1976 and FK Austria in 1978, Robbie Rensenbrink scoring twice each time. The now-famous mauve-and-whites won the UEFA Cup in 1983 and lost it only on penalties to Tottenham in the 1984 final.

BARCELONA

Barcelona take a photo-call at the start of the 1984–5 season; Steve Archibald (ex-Spurs) is in the centre of the front row. Probably the world's wealthiest club, and in Spain second in prestige only to Real Madrid.

*C*atalonians would like to believe that Barcelona is now in its third great postwar period, one that could even surpass those of 1945–53 and 1957–60.

In the first of these periods the club achieved five League championships and a hat trick (1951–3) of Spanish Cup wins. In the second Barcelona emerged from Real's giant shadow to take the first two Fairs' Cups, then successive League titles (1959 and 1960), and reach the 1961 European Cup final after knocking out Real.

A team boasting the forward line of Ladislav Kubala, Sándor Kocsis, Juan de Macedo Evaristo, Luis Suarez and Zoltán Czibor managed to lose that 1961 final to Benfica and, amazingly, could win only two Spanish League titles in the next 25 years.

One came in 1974 when the ban on foreign players was lifted and Barcelona's enormous resources funded the purchase of Johan Cruyff. Then after another frustrating wait Terry Venables replaced coach César Menotti, sold Diego Maradona and won the League by 10 clear points. Failure to capture the 1986 European Cup from Steaua Bucharest did not diminish his popularity.

DYNAMO MOSCOW

*B*orn as Morozovtsi, a team drawn from textile mills who won the Moscow championship for five successive years, Dynamo Moscow adopted its present name in 1923, having become the electrical trade union team.

In October 1945, as Soviet champions, Dynamo was chosen to make a tour of Britain that attracted enormous interest and considerable controversy. An estimated 100,000 (15,000 above official capacity) turned up to see Dynamo's first game with Chelsea (3–3); in Scotland the Russians held the leading club Glasgow Rangers (2–2); in Wales Cardiff City was beaten 10–1; and back in London a specially strengthened Arsenal team went down 4–3, Dynamo managing to play in the thick fog with 12 men for some 20 minutes. It was following this tour that George Orwell was moved to make his famous comment that 'Sport is an unfailing cause of ill-will.'

Had Orwell been alive in 1972, he would doubtless have sighed as another meeting of Dynamo and Rangers – in the European Cup Winners' Cup final – was marred by clashes between Rangers supporters and the Barcelona police. Dynamo lost 3–2 and has struggled ever since to become a force once more, even in its own country.

FERENCVÁROS HAMBURG

England striker Kevin Keegan, signed from Liverpool in 1977 by SV Hamburg's new manager, the great midfielder Günter Netzer, helped the German club to success in the Bundesliga and to the final of the European Cup.

Few great clubs have been taken over by another and later resumed their own identity. That happened to Ferencváros after the Second World War.

One of the oldest and most successful clubs in Hungary – formed in 1899 and champions by 1903 – Ferencváros was completely subsumed by the army team Honvéd, who already had one Ferenc Puskás and was able to incorporate Sándor Kocsis and Zoltán Czibor into a brilliant forward line. However,

after the revolution of 1956 'Fradi' was able to assume its own identity again.

Florian Albert, gifted centre-forward and fine leader, was the star of the next successful Ferencváros side, which between 1963 and 1968 won the League four times and reached two Fairs' Cups finals – beating Juventus on its own ground in 1965, but losing over two legs to Leeds three years later.

In the 1970s, however, Ferencváros had to take a back seat

at home as Ujpesti Dózsa completed seven successive Hungarian championships.

Had there been a genuine national League in West Germany before 1963, Hamburg might have benefited more than any other club, for its domination of the northern regional League (Oberliga Nord) was almost total. In the 29 competitions played between 1921 and 1963 Hamburg finished top no fewer than 25 times, frequently reaching 100 goals in a season's 30 matches.

Many of these goals from 1954 onwards were scored by Uwe Seeler, the short and stocky centre-forward who played in four World Cups, two of them (1966 and 1970) as captain. He it was who was instrumental in Hamburg's winning the West German championship in 1960 and a European Cup semifinal place the

following year (when the side lost only on a play-off to Barcelona).

Kevin Keegan, signed from Liverpool in 1977, helped the team win the Bundesliga in his second season, which was followed by a narrow European Cup final defeat against Nottingham Forest.

A remarkable unbeaten run of 36 games between January 1982 and January 1983 was the backbone of two further championship successes and in May 1983 the club became European champions at last when Felix Magath's goal beat Juventus in the final.

ST-ETIENNE

St-Etienne (green strip) take on Bayern Munich in the European Cup final of 1976, which Bayern won 1–0. A major force in French football in the 1970s, St-Etienne's dominance has now passed to clubs like Bordeaux, Monaco and Paris St-Germain.

Most of the excitement in St-Etienne's history has been contained in the period between 1962 and 1984 which both began and ended with relegation to the second division.

St-Etienne leaped straight back in 1963, winning the French Cup even as the club was demoted and taking the first division title at the first attempt. Goalkeeper Pierre Bernard and all-rounder Robert Herbin were regulars in the national team and Herbin was still prominent as the revered Albert Batteux returned to lead *les Verts* to four successive titles from 1967 to 1970.

Herbin was coach for the next outstanding run – a hat trick of championships and some success at last in Europe. In the 1974–5 European Cup St-Etienne overcame a 4–1 deficit from the away leg against Hajduk Split, only to lose in the semifinal to Bayern Munich, who defeated the French side 1–0 in the following year's final.

The Revelli brothers, Hervé and Patrick, Dominique Bathenay, Jean Michel Larqué and Dominique Rocheteau were well-respected names from that side. Michel Platini and Patrick Battiston were later recruited, but the illegal payments scandal of 1982 was followed by relegation and the need to rebuild the side again.

TOTTENHAM HOTSPUR

It is a tradition in North London that Spurs win something when the year ends in a '1': 1901 and 1921 the FA Cup; 1951 the League; 1961 the rare League and Cup double; 1971 the Football League Cup; 1981 the FA Cup.

Bill Nicholson was manager during the 1960s when Tottenham briefly supplanted Manchester United and Wolves as England's top club. In tandem with Northern Ireland's captain Danny Blanchflower he built a team which reached the European Cup semifinal, unluckily losing to Benfica, and then thrashed Atlético 5–1 in the 1963 Cup Winners' Cup final, even without the inspirational wing-half Dave Mackay.

Hitting a low point after defeat in the 1974 UEFA Cup final and Nicholson's resignation, Tottenham signed Argentinian World Cup players Ossie Ardiles and Ricardo Villa, and when Steve Archibald and Garth Crooks were signed to finish off their work, the FA Cup was won in successive seasons (1981 and 1982) and the UEFA Cup on penalties in 1984.

ABERDEEN

The Glasgow duopoly of Celtic and Rangers, which had dominated Scottish football for almost 90 years, was suddenly shattered as the 1980s began by two clubs from the east of the country: Aberdeen and Dundee United.

In 1979–80 the promise they had shown under dynamic managers Alex Ferguson and Jim McLean was amply realized.

Aberdeen overhauled Celtic in a dramatic finish to win only its second championship with a team containing Steve Archibald (later to play for Tottenham Hotspur and Barcelona); Gordon Strachan (Manchester United); and Mark McGhee (Hamburg).

The League runners-up in 1981 and 1982, Aberdeen then achieved a hat trick of Scottish Cup victories and scored an exciting extra-time win over Real Madrid in the 1983 European Cup Winners' Cup final. A domestic League and Cup double followed in 1984 (the first by any club other than Celtic and Rangers) and even after selling Strachan Aberdeen retained the League title in 1985.

The balance of power in Scottish football had changed for the first time.

ARSENAL

Viv Anderson, Arsenal's tall and leggy right-back, was the first black player to command a regular place in the England squad, where in recent years he has kept company with fellow Gunners Kenny Sansom and Tony Woodcock.

A remarkably famous name throughout the world of football for a club whose achievements since the Second World War have been comparatively few.

That name was made in the 1930s by winning the League or FA Cup seven times in nine seasons. The counter-attacking style refined by the innovative Herbert Chapman (who died in 1934) did not make the Gunners popular winners, as was again the case when they recorded a rare

English League and Cup double in 1971. Nine years later Arsenal became the first team to lose a European final on penalties (the Cup Winners' Cup to Valencia).

ATLÉTICO MADRID

Always the poor relation of Real Madrid, Atlético has normally managed a couple of domestic League and Cup wins each decade plus an occasional European sortie – just enough to keep the fans at the Vicente Calderón stadium hoping, but not enough to save the jobs of a series of coaches.

The European Cup Winners' Cup was won in 1962, breaking a long run (1951–66) without a Spanish League title, but lost to Tottenham Hotspur in 1963.

The 1974 European Cup final was ruined when Bayern Munich scored a last-minute equalizer, before winning the replay 4–0. The football world is more likely to remember the semifinal against Glasgow Celtic when Atlético had three players sent off and four others booked.

BOCA JUNIORS · BORDEAUX

Emigrant Italians living in one of the poorest areas of Buenos Aires formed Boca Juniors in 1905 and, once professionalism was established and the rival Argentinian Leagues merged into one, the club was prominent for two decades.

A spell of 18 years with only one national title was ended in 1962 and Boca became the first Argentinian side to reach the South American Clubs Cup final, where Pelé's Santos just beat them.

However, the team that won three South American titles in a row from 1977 will be remembered principally for some of the wild matches it was involved in. Not a single Boca player was included in Argentina's World Cup squad of 1978 because manager Menotti felt they were too big a risk.

Bordeaux's Pichon (centre) gets past two Fenerbahçe defenders in the first round of the 1986 European Cup, when the Girondins inexplicably lost 2–3 at home to the Turkish champions.

The Girondins of Bordeaux were about to celebrate their centenary with just one French championship victory behind them when an aggressive policy of buying paid off and made this the country's leading team.

A whole clutch of internationals – Bernard Lacombe, Patrick Battiston, Marius Trésor, Dieter Müller and Caspar Memering among them – came to join Alain Giresse and they were joined in

1981 by Jean Tigana.

Runners-up in 1983 (two years after the centenary), the Girondins took the championship the following year and retained it 12 months later after another bold signing – Fernando Chalana from Benfica for a national record fee of £1.5 million.

BORUSSIA MÖNCHENGLADBACH

Borussia meant nothing in West German football when the Bundesliga began in 1963. The previous season the club had finished 11th in its regional league, only four points clear of relegation. But within a decade Borussia was in the final of a major European competition.

Coach Hennes Weisweiler, who joined the club in 1964, must take most of the credit.

He took Borussia into the Bundesliga within two seasons and by 1970 the Mönchengladbacher were champions – going on to win five titles in eight seasons (Bayern took the other three).

Despite two UEFA Cup triumphs, the club's highest ambitions in the European Cup were cruelly frustrated. It lost on penalties to Everton in the first campaign; then to Inter

Milan after a 7–1 home win was annulled because Roberto Boninsegna had been struck by a drinks can; third time out came defeat by Real on away goals; then by Liverpool in the 1977 final and 1978 semifinal!

It was poor reward for players like Bertie Vogts, Rainer Bonhof, Günter Netzer, then later Allan Simonsen and Uli Stielike.

DYNAMO KIEV

It took 25 years for anyone other than Moscow clubs to win the Soviet Union's championship. Then Kiev took the 1961 title and can claim to have been the outstanding team over the quarter-century that followed.

Champions ten times more between 1966 and 1985, the Kiev men were also their country's first winners of a big European competition, beating Ferencváros in the 1975 Cup Winners' Cup, and went on to defeat European champions Bayern in the 'Super Cup'. Another first in that season for Soviet football was the election of the Kiev outside-left Oleg Blokhin as European Footballer of the Year.

Playing important European games outside the Russians' normal season has tended to handicap Kiev as much as any other Soviet team, and in the European Cup itself the club's best achievement was a semifinal place in 1977. But in 1986, with Blokhin still going strong, the club again won the Cup Winners' Cup.

EVERTON

Everton's team photographed before the European Cup-Winners' Cup final of 1985, when they beat Rapid Vienna 3–1. Everton owe much of their recent success to the shrewdness of manager Howard Kendall and to the flair of coach Colin Harvey — both brilliant half-backs for the team in the late 1960s.

Previously overshadowed by neighbours Liverpool, and with a mediocre record in Europe, Everton suddenly blossomed in the 1980s.

Everton's manager Howard Kendall had been a wing-half in the previous championship-winning side of 1970, which reached the European Cup quarter-final before losing to the unfancied Greek club Panathinaikos.

That was the only occasion on which the club had reached the last eight in nine attempts until 1985 – when Everton brushed aside Bayern Munich in the Cup Winners' Cup

semifinal and Rapid Vienna in the final.

The club's most famous player of earlier generations was William 'Dixie' Dean, whose 60 League goals in 1927–8 (100 in all matches) is unlikely ever to be beaten.

FEYENOORD

Like Ajax, Rotterdam's Feyenoord built slowly following the introduction of professionalism in Holland, eventually becoming champions not only of Europe but, in 1970, of the world.

Under coach Ernst Happel Feyenoord beat Iceland's KR Reykjavik 16–2 on aggregate, put out the holders Milan and returned to Milan's San Siro stadium to win the final against Glasgow Celtic in extra time – Swedish striker Ove Kindvall scored the winning goal.

The club was then overtaken by Ajax again, managing only a UEFA Cup win in 1974. And even Feyenoord's first League title for a decade in 1984 was achieved thanks to Cruyff, sensationally signed from rival Ajax before he returned there as coach.

FK AUSTRIA

The Vienna Cricket and Football Club was the forefather of FK Austria, whose more recent name changes have included: Austria/WAC (after amalgamating with Wiener AC in 1973); Austria/Vienna in 1981, which did not interrupt a run of four successive championships; and then FK Austria Memphis as the badly needed sponsors were given some additional prominence.

Throughout it all the side has vied with Rapid Vienna as Austria's leading club, winning fewer League titles but with greater success in Europe. FK Austria reached the 1978 Cup Winners' Cup final and the 1979 European Cup semifinal, losing to the defensive Swedish strategists of Malmö 1–0 on aggregate.

FLAMENGO

Zico, in the red and black of Flamengo, whose move to Italian football with Udinese dismayed the club's supporters and allowed Fluminense to become Rio's top club again. He returned late in 1985.

The Flamengo–Fluminense (Fla–Flu) rivalry in former Brazilian capital Rio de Janeiro matches that of any other clubs in the world and can still draw crowds of 150,000 to the Maracana stadium when they meet. It is all the keener because Flamengo was founded in 1911 by disenchanted Fluminense members. By 1915 Flamengo had twice won the Rio championship, and later achieved hat tricks in 1942–4 and 1953–5.

The most notable player was Leonidas da Silva, 'the Black Diamond', who was at his best between signing from Botafogo in 1936 and moving to

São Paulo in 1942.

Zico became the star attraction of modern times, leading the team to three national championships, and in 1981 to the South American Clubs Cup and the World Clubs Cup with an emphatic 3–0 win over Liverpool in Tokyo. Supporters were stunned when he left for Italy in 1983, but thrilled to welcome him back in 1985 with fellow Brazilian superstar Socrates.

FLUMINENSE

English emigrant Oscar Cox helped found Fluminense in 1902, oldest of the Brazilian clubs started for soccer as opposed to sailing (like Flamengo and Vasco de Gama).

Winning five of the first six Rio de Janeiro titles, Fluminense reigned for long periods, but once a national championship began in 1967 the club found it difficult to win. One success in 1970 was followed by a long wait until 1984, after which Carlos Alberto (captain of the 1970 World Cup winners) became coach.

With the Paraguayan midfielder Julio César Romero outstanding, Fluminense did at least exert some superiority over the Zico-less Flamengo by winning the Rio title again in 1983, 1984 and 1985.

GLASGOW CELTIC

Celtic players mob Gemmell after he equalized in the 1967 European Cup final at Lisbon.

Formed in 1887 to play friendly matches for Catholic charities, it is an irony – though a heartening one, given Glasgow's sectarian background – that the most influential figure in Celtic's history has been a Protestant, Jock Stein (1923–85). He it was who finally lifted the side one step above Glasgow Rangers, the eternal enemy in one of those rivalries common to great soccer cities.

By 1965, when Stein returned to Parkhead as manager, Rangers led by 33 championship wins to 20. Starting in his first full season, Celtic reeled off nine successive titles to redress the balance a little. More important, Celtic became the first British club to win the European Cup when in 1967 goals by full-back Tommy Gemmell and centre-forward Steve Chalmers undid Inter, the kings of defensive *catenaccio* play.

Losing to Argentina's Racing Club in the World Clubs' Cup when six players were sent

off, Celtic reached another European final three years later, only to lose to Feyenoord as a familiar Scottish over-confidence took hold.

GLASGOW RANGERS

Founded in 1873, Glasgow Rangers had won only two Scottish championships (one shared) by the turn of the century, but made up for it afterwards and still stand second only to Peñarol for the greatest number of national championships won in any country. Rangers were simply untouchable between the two wars, winning 15 titles in 21 years;

but, like many other great clubs, they were unpleasantly surprised later by European competition.

In the European Cup there were setbacks like Milan's 4–1 win at Ibrox and the 12–4 aggregate humiliation by Eintracht Frankfurt, a team who in turn conceded seven in the subsequent Glasgow final.

The Cup Winners'

Cup brought two defeats in finals, by Fiorentina and Bayern Munich, and even the triumph of 1972 led to a ban because of the Rangers supporters' wild behaviour.

Ibrox Park, now quite spectacularly modernized, has been the scene of two serious crowd disasters: 25 spectators were killed at a match against Celtic in 1902, and 66

died at another such derby on New Year's Day 1971.

INDEPENDIENTE

While often considered inferior to the other great Buenos Aires clubs like Boca and River Plate, the Independiente men have established a remarkable record in the South American Cup and twice been world champions.

Independiente's

success in the 1960s was based on the *catenaccio*-style defence which brought the club South American championships against Uruguay's Nacional (1964) and Peñarol (1965), so it was appropriate that Inter, perfectors of the style, should defeat the side

each time in the World Clubs Cup.

Later, however, in 1972–5 came a run that may never be equalled: four successive South American titles, and the side's first World Clubs victory when Independiente defeated Juventus in Italy. And in December 1984 the club

beat Liverpool 1–0 in Tokyo with a team captained by the former Nantes defender Enzo Trossero.

NACIONAL

Together he Nacional club is the perpetual rival of Peñarol in Montevideo, the first South American city to provide two different World Club champions. Nacional won the title in 1971, during its second golden period.

The previous such period was 1939–48, when there were five successive Uruguayan championships earned by the great goal-scoring power of the Argentinian star Atilio García.

In 1980, unlike 1971, Nacional had to defeat the genuine European champions to win the World Clubs Cup: Waldemar Victorino's goal beat Nottingham Forest.

NANTES

Comparative newcomer among the top French clubs, Brittany's Nantes did not reach the first division until 1963 – but took the championship within two seasons.

Jacques Simon's 24 goals pushed the club towards that first title and another the following year. As St-Etienne took over in later years, Nantes was restricted to a victory in the championship every three years or so – in 1973, 1977, 1980 and 1983 – without achieving anything in Europe other than a semifinal place in the 1980 Cup Winners' Cup, when the Bretons succumbed to Mario

Kempes and Valencia.

In half a dozen European Cups Nantes has won barely one tie per year, once losing to Vejle of Denmark, as well as to more established clubs such as Atlético Madrid (1966), Glasgow Celtic (1967) and Inter Milan (1981).

Central defender Yvon Le Roux of Nantes and France was sent off in the final of the 1984 European Championship against Spain. Previously with Brest and Monaco, he also made the 1986 World Cup squad but appeared only in the third-place match against Belgium.

PEÑAROL

As the winners of its national championship more times than any other club in the world, it was appropriate that Peñarol should be South America's first official champions when the Libertadores Cup began in 1960. Although beaten heavily by Real Madrid in the World

Clubs tie that followed, the Uruguayan club had its revenge by defeating Benfica the following year and, indeed, Real itself in the 1966 competition.

Victory over Aston Villa in 1982 then made Peñarol the first club to be crowned world champions three times.

The 1985 Uruguayan

League title was the club's 39th, though on that occasion Peñarol was almost banned from competing in the South American Cup because its players had not been paid. Financial problems remain acute in Montevideo, a city of only 1.3 millions trying to support two of the world's great clubs.

RAPID VIENNA

Rapid Vienna's squad pictured before being roundly defeated by Everton in the 1985 Cup Winners' Cup final in Rotterdam. Stars of this side were the two ageing maestros Hans Krankl and Antonín Panenka.

Not many clubs can have won the championship of two countries. Rapid Vienna, already the outstanding Austrian team when the country was annexed by Hitler in 1938, proceeded to win the German Cup a year later, and then the 1941 German championship.

Despite appearing frequently in European competition, Rapid suffered a long spell without winning the Austrian League between 1968 and 1982, all the more remarkable in that the side's centre-forward during the 1970s was the country's best-known player, Hans Krankl.

He joined Barcelona after the 1978 World Cup, but was back for the controversial Cup Winners' Cup run of 1984–5 when UEFA ordered the match against Celtic to be replayed: Rapid went on to the final against Everton, Krankl scoring in the 3–1 defeat.

RED STAR BELGRADE

Yugoslavia's most successful club was not formed until 1945, in the big reorganization which followed the Second World War.

Then a hat trick of domestic Cup wins from 1948 to 1950 announced Red Star's arrival and was followed by championship wins in 1951 and 1953, when spectacular goalkeeper Vladimir Beara was the star turn.

Red Star might well have reached the second European Cup final in 1957: Fiorentina squeezed past the Yugoslavs only 1–0 on aggregate. Miljan Miljanic built another fine team in the mid-1970s, one that stunned Liverpool in the same competition with home and away victories.

The side did reach a European final, the UEFA Cup, in 1979, losing narrowly to Mönchengladbach after 87,500 had watched Red Star's home leg. Such large crowds are still common for important European games.

RIVER PLATE

Although it is not immune from the financial problems that afflict the other Argentinian clubs, River Plate can at least count on the country's best attendances, with more than 50,000 thronging through its gates for the big Buenos Aires derbies.

The club's great stadium was built at the end of the 1930s, a lucrative and successful decade, when River Plate's goal scorer Bernabe Ferreyra was Argentina's star.

Later came the great Di Stéfano and then Daniel Passarella, captain of Argentina's World Cup-winning team and a River Plate stalwart from 1972 to 1982 before moving to Fiorentina. A new hero was imported in Enzo Francescoli, the Uruguayan midfielder who was voted South American Footballer of the Year in 1984.

SANTOS

Pelé, the most famous — and probably the greatest — footballer in history, made Santos the most successful Brazilian club side in the 1960s. A complete master of all the arts of both midfielder and striker, Pelé scored over 1000 goals in his professional career.

Once Pelé had retired it took almost ten years for the club he made famous to have any significant impact again, even in Brazil. In 1984 the goals of Serginho brought them the state championship again, in front of 100,000 fans, but there was still no South American Cup place.

Pelé signed as a 15-year-old in 1955 and a fine team built around him included Claudio Coutinho at centre-forward, Zito in midfield and the left-winger with the similar name of Pepé. Santos was at its peak as Brazil retained the 1962 World Cup, and devastated Benfica 3–2 in São Paulo and then 5–2 in Lisbon to win the World Clubs Cup.

Santos regularly played vast numbers of matches, with friendlies all over Europe, but in consequence perhaps had surprisingly few other trophies to show off by the time Pelé called it a day.

SPORTING LISBON

The great Sporting team that won seven League titles in eight seasons from 1947 to 1954 was just past its peak when European competition began. But the club will hold for ever the distinction of staging the first-ever European Cup match, which took place at its José Alvalade stadium on 4 September 1955: a 3–3 draw against Partizan Belgrade (who won the second leg 5–2).

Although Benfica soon became the main Portuguese force, Sporting won the championship again every fourth year in a remarkable sequence: 1958, 1962, 1966, 1970 and 1974.

Sporting Lisbon also took the Cup Winners' Cup in 1964, beating Apoel Nicosia by 16–1, a European record, in Lisbon *en route*.

STADE DE REIMS

Nobody can take away the glory earned by Stade de Reims between 1949 and 1962, but as that great period slips further back into the past, the club's dwindling company of supporters cannot seriously contemplate any repeat.

Albert Batteux captained Reims to a first French national championship win in 1949, and was coach for the first European Cup of 1956 when with Raymond Kopa, Just Fontaine and centre-half Robert Jonquet all outstanding, the side reached and lost a truly epic final against Real Madrid.

Three years later Kopa was on the opposite side as Real beat Reims again in the final, but he returned to inspire further championship success in 1960 and 1962. When Batteux was allowed to leave in 1963, however, relegation followed and one of Europe's great clubs was reduced to near bankruptcy.

B ECKENBAUER

C HARLTON CRUYFF

D IDÍ

FRANZ BECKENBAUER

Born 11 September 1945 in Munich, West Germany, *der Kaiser* was originally a forward and prodigious goal scorer, who would later play in midfield for the national team (he was outstanding in the 1966 World Cup aged only 20) and as *Libero* (sweeper) for Bayern Munich. Captained West Germany to its European Championship victory in 1972 and the World Cup two years later; and Bayern to a hat trick of European Cups. After winning 103 caps between 1965 and 1977 he left for New York Cosmos, and eventually took over as team manager of West Germany.

GEORGE BEST

Born 22 May 1946 in Belfast, Northern Ireland, a supremely gifted winger with an instinct for self-destruction. Joined Manchester United at the age of 15 and at 17 was a first-team regular alongside Charlton and Law as well as a Northern Ireland international. Good looks and a Beatle haircut made him a 1960s 'showbiz' celebrity, too, but from Manchester United's European Cup win in 1968 it was all downhill via a succession of clubs and, in 1981, a clinic for alcoholics. Still plays enthusiastically in charity matches all over Britain.

BOBBY CHARLTON

Born 11 October 1937, Bobby Charlton was a boy star who became England's most popular football ambassador after surviving the horrific Munich air disaster of 1958. Played on either wing or at centre-forward, then in midfield, totalling 106 caps and a record 49 goals for England. Played 753 League and Cup games for Manchester United (246 goals), plus a handful for Preston with whom he unsuccessfully tried management.

JOHAN CRUYFF

Outstanding figure in the Ajax and Dutch national teams which rivalled Bayern and West Germany as Europe's, if not the world's, best in the mid-1970s. A beautiful athlete, much more powerful on the ground and in the air than his lean frame suggested, he was voted European Footballer of the Year in 1971, 1973 and 1974. Played in four European Cup finals for Ajax before leading the Dutch exodus to Spain, when he joined and revitalized Barcelona. Returned to Holland to Feyenoord, then to his great love Ajax, where he became coach.

DIDÍ

Born Walter Pereira in 1928, the brilliant midfield orchestrator of Brazil's 1958 and 1962 World Cup winning teams – aged 30 and then 34. One of the earliest and most talented exponents of the 'banana kick', he briefly left Botafogo for Real Madrid in 1959, but could not combine with Alfredo Di Stéfano and returned home. Coach to the exciting Peruvian team which lost to his own country in the quarter-final of the 1970 World Cup.

D ISTÉFANO

E USEBIO

F ONTAINE

G ARRINCHA
ENTO

ALFREDO DI STÉFANO

In the opinion of many good judges, the greatest all-round player of all. A centre-forward who could not only score goals, but would glide all over the field, doing any job that had to be done with total assurance. Born 1926 in Buenos Aires, Argentina, he played for River Plate, then in the outlawed Colombian League before Real Madrid secured him in 1953. For 11 years he was the dominant figure there, scoring in each of the first five European Cup finals. Left for Español amid some acrimony, later coaching Valencia (twice), Real and Boca Juniors.

EUSEBIO

Eusebio da Silva Ferreira followed Mario Coluna from his native Mozambique to Benfica of Lisbon, where both were key figures in Portugal's finest decade. Won only one of his four European Cup finals (scoring twice in the defeat of Real Madrid in 1962), but totalled 46 goals in the competition and was top scorer in the 1966 World Cup finals.

JUST FONTAINE

Scorer of a record 13 goals for France in the World Cup finals of 1958, where he might not have played at all if team mate René Bliard had not injured an ankle. He was re-united with former Reims colleague Raymond Kopa to devastating effect, scoring in every match. Great

acceleration and shooting power – although he once said, 'I wish I had the class of Kopa.'

GARRINCHA

The 'little bird' whose shooting with both feet and body swerve were all the more remarkable in that he had been semi-crippled as a child. Bursting on to the scene with Pelé when Brazilian team mates demanded his inclusion late in the 1958 World Cup, he was voted Player of the Tournament in 1962, but was past his best by 1966 when he was still recovering from a car crash.

FRANCISCO GENTO

Probably the fastest winger in the world during the late 1950s, certainly the longest-serving of all Real Madrid's top players. Signed from Santander for £7000 just before Alfredo Di Stéfano in 1953, he played in a record 88 European Cup ties, including no fewer than eight finals between 1956 and 1966. Also added an appearance in the 1971 Cup Winners' Cup final just before retirement.

BECKENBAUER · GENTO

HIDEGKUTI KOPA LAW MATTHEWS MOORE

NÁNDOR HIDEGKUTI

The original deep-lying centre-forward in Hungary's magnificent team of 1950–5. Not only made vast numbers of goals for Puskás and Kocsis, homing in on his passes after the centre-half was lured out of position, but was quite likely to score himself from any distance. Unlike Ferenc Puskás, returned to Hungary from Honvéd's tour when the 1956 revolution broke out, but was beginning to flounder by the 1958 World Cup.

RAYMOND KOPA

Born Raymond Kopażewski, the son of a Polish miner, he was indisputably France's greatest footballer until the advent of Michel Platini. Began with Angers, then starred in the Reims side that was only just beaten in the first European Cup final by Real Madrid, who had already agreed to sign him. Moved from centre-forward to outside-right, he played in Real's next three European triumphs before returning to France, temporarily for the 1958 World Cup, and permanently with Reims again.

DENIS LAW

Manchester United had Bobby Charlton and George Best. But it was the club's third European Footballer of the Year, Denis Law, who supporters called 'The King'. He rewarded them with 171 League goals in 309 games after signing from Torino in 1962 – then scored the goal

that relegated Manchester United from Division One after joining neighbour and enemy Manchester City. Scored 30 goals in 55 internationals for Scotland.

SIR STANLEY MATTHEWS

characterized it. 'Stan' was 38 when he finally gained an FA Cup Winners' medal at Wembley; 42 when awarded the last of his 54 international caps; 46 when he rejoined his first club Stoke City; and 50 when he played his last League match. Rarely a goal scorer and ineffective in the air – yet still one of the greatest players of all time.

Born on 1 February 1915, the longevity of Matthews' career was as extraordinary as the dribbling that

BOBBY MOORE

World Cup final when his passes made two of Geoff Hurst's three goals. Finished his career with Fulham in 1976 and briefly became a Football League manager with Southend.

Born 12 April 1941 in East London, an icily efficient central defender for West Ham (1958–73) who became England's most capped player, making his 108th and last appearance in 1974. He was England's captain for ten years, including the 1966

M ÜLLER
P ELÉ
USKÁS
Y ASHIN
Z OFF

GERD MÜLLER

Joined Bayern Munich from TSV Nördlingen in

1963 to help Franz Beckenbauer inspire a wonderful period for club and country. Scored 365 goals in the Bundesliga and 68 in 62 internationals: a phenomenal rate in modern soccer. Never one for spectacular long-range shots, he was unequalled around the six-yard box.

PELÉ

Born 21 October 1940, Edson Arantes do Nascimento was given at an early age the name of Pelé, which would

become the most famous that football has ever known. The world at large first became aware of it when he was thrust into the 1958 World Cup, aged 17, scoring six goals in the last three games; by 1970 he had 1000 to his credit. Retirement from international soccer was followed by a comeback in the United States, a great coup for the New York Cosmos.

FERENC PUSKÁS

Born 1927, the tubby, left-footed Hungarian

army officer enjoyed two distinct football careers. Firstly, theoretically as an amateur, with Honvéd and Hungary, Olympic champions of 1952 but amazingly beaten in the 1954 World Cup final when he was not fully fit; then, after idling away 18 months following the 1956 Hungarian uprising, at Real Madrid as foil to Alfredo Di Stéfano in soccer's greatest double act. He even appeared

in Spain's unsuccessful 1962 World Cup team, and played his last European Cup tie at the age of 38. Later coached Panathinaikos to the 1971 final and AEK Athens to the Greek championship.

LEV YASHIN

The best of all goalkeepers? Certainly a contender. Yashin, born in 1929, was the only keeper to win the European Footballer of the Year award – an

honour he received in 1963 after playing for the Rest of the World XI at Wembley. Having decided to concentrate on football rather than ice hockey with Dynamo Moscow, he won an Olympics gold in 1956 and played in the first two European Championship finals as well as three World Cups. Even in 1970 was still in the Soviet squad, aged 40, but did not add to his 78 caps.

DINO ZOFF

Born 28 February 1942, Italy's goalkeeper Zoff was 40 years and 4 months old when he lifted the World Cup in Madrid in 1982 after his country's victory over West Germany – his 106th appearance. As a

teenager he had been turned down by several Italian clubs, then joined Udinese in 1962, later moving on to Mantova (Mantua), Napoli and Juventus. Unbeaten for 10 successive matches with 'Juve', he surpassed that at international level by not conceding a goal in 12 matches, or 1143 minutes, between 1972 and 1974: quite a record even for a man playing behind traditionally well-populated Italian defences.

B RADY
BRIEGEL

D ALGLISH
DASSAYEV

F ALCÃO

LIAM BRADY

Seventh child of a Dublin sporting family, 'Chippy' Brady followed two brothers into English soccer, starring in the Arsenal team that reached three successive FA Cup finals and lost the 1980 European Cup Winners' final on penalties. Although he is predominantly a midfield creator, he scored 59 goals for the club and has been in great demand ever since; Juventus, Sampdoria and Inter each secured his services for two years.

HANS-PETER BRIEGEL

A former decathlete who went into the European Championship finals of 1980 as a reserve with three caps and came out a star. Following the 1982 World Cup he left an unfashionable West German club (Kaiserslautern) for an unfashionable Italian one (Verona) and helped it to its first-ever championship title. A fearsome competitor, whether at full-back or in midfield, who intimidates with his sheer physical presence.

KENNY DALGLISH

Born 4 March 1951, Kenny Dalglish left a starring role with Glasgow Celtic for what looked a difficult part as Kevin Keegan's successor at Liverpool. He was an immediate success, going on to become the second player to score 100 League goals in both England and Scotland. By 1986 he had not only become the first Scot to win 100 caps, and his country's joint highest-ever scorer, but had taken over as Liverpool's first player-manager, leading the club to an extraordinary League and Cup double in his first season.

RINAT DASSAYEV

A worthy successor to the great Lev Yashin, even if he does play for Moscow rivals Spartak rather than Dynamo. Yashin's record of 75 caps has now become an obvious target for a man generally considered to be among the top two or three goalkeepers in the world. Dassayev has frequently captained the USSR.

PAOLO ROBERTO FALCÃO

Born in 1953, a star with Internacional of Pôrto Alegre, whom he drove to five state titles and three Brazilian championships. Roma paid £950,000 to take him to Italy in 1980 and was rewarded with the League title and a European Cup final appearance as well. Outstanding for Brazil in the 1982 World Cup, he returned there with São Paulo in 1985.

GIRESSE GOMES LAUDRUP MARADONA OLSEN

ALAIN GIRESSE

Bordeaux and France who nevertheless took a long time to achieve his international prominence. Despite winning his first cap in 1974, aged 21, his talents were only recognized outside his own country after a brilliant 1982 World Cup, by which time Bordeaux was building a splendid team around him.

Outstanding little midfielder with

FERNANDO GOMES

native Portugal and FC Porto has every reason to be grateful. A successful centre-forward with that club since the age of 15, he had topped the Portuguese scoring list in 1977, 1978 and 1979. Then, returning from Spain, he won the 'Golden Boot' as Europe's leading scorer with 36 in 1983 and 39 two years later.

An unhappy two-year spell in Spain with Gijón convinced Gomes that his future lay in his

MICHAEL LAUDRUP

decided to leave the little Danish club Brøndby (managed by his father). He turned down Barcelona and Liverpool to sign for Juventus, who loaned him to Lazio in Rome for two valuable years. He was then ready to play at the highest level and whether in attack for Denmark, or slightly withdrawn with Juventus, he has looked an outstanding player in any company.

The most sought-after youngster in Europe when, in 1983, he

DIEGO MARADONA

A full international shortly after his 16th birthday, Maradona was mortified to be left out of Argentina's 1978 World Cup squad when he might have made the same kind of impact as Pelé at a similar age. Government assistance with finance helped keep him in Argentina – but nobody could prevent him leaving for Barcelona for a staggering £5 million. Later Napoli would pay even more for a talent rare in any era.

Those with any doubts about his ability or temperament surely had them removed at the 1986 World Cup finals

where he lifted Argentina into the final with a clutch of goals, notably one virtuoso dribble from his own half to score against England. An astute pass for Burruchaga then produced a winning goal against West Germany just when it seemed that Maradona and his team would have the Cup snatched away from them. The finals illustrated his many gifts: pace and strength on the ball, irrepressible dribbling ability, a tremendous shot, and a new, more mature demeanour as captain.

JESPER OLSEN

either wide in attack or in midfield. He was one of Ajax's many Danish imports, joining Manchester United in 1984 and settling in to become one of few successful foreign players in the English Football League.

Næstved was the first club of this waspish player who can operate

BRADY · OLSEN

4

PLATINI

ROBSON
ROSSI
RUMMENIGGE

RUSH

MICHEL PLATINI

Born 21 June 1955 with Italian godparents, which made Italy a natural choice once St-Etienne had gone as far as it seemed likely to in 1982. He had totalled 156 goals in 262 French League games for Nancy and St-Etienne, and continued scoring at a remarkable rate in the tighter confines of Italian football with 'Juve' – demonstrating the striking ability of a complete modern midfield player. Voted European Footballer of the Year on a record three successive occasions (1983–5), Platini also overtook Just Fontaine's French international scoring record to earn comparisons with Kopa as his country's finest-ever player.

BRYAN ROBSON

'Pop' Robson became Britain's most expensive player when his former manager Ron Atkinson took him from West Bromwich Albion to Manchester United for £1.5 million in October 1981, 18 months after his England debut. A dynamic midfielder and goal scorer who could easily play in defence – where he might sustain less damage. A series of injuries to him left England under a cloud going into the 1986 World Cup finals.

PAOLO ROSSI

Italy's hero of the 1982 World Cup when he returned from a two-year suspension to devastate Argentina, Brazil, Poland and West Germany. Six goals in all made him the tournament's top scorer and also European Footballer of the Year. A Vicenza player when making his mark in the previous World Cup, he was loaned to Perugia and became involved in a match-fixing scandal – though he strongly protested his innocence. Juventus bought him for £500,000, and then controversially sold him to Milan after winning the 1985 European Cup.

KARL-HEINZ RUMMENIGGE

Born 25 September 1955, 'Rummi' was a promising youngster in the Bayern Munich team that completed a hat trick of European Cup wins in 1976. He stayed for another eight years, scoring 162 Bundesliga goals and captaining West Germany to the 1980 European Championship. In 1984, even at the age of almost 29, Inter Milan was prepared to make him Europe's most expensive player ever at a figure of £3 million and he responded enthusiastically to the challenge of Italian soccer.

IAN RUSH

Like Liam Brady, a home-loving man from a big family who has become a world star without ever appearing in the European Championship or World Cup finals. Liverpool paid £300,000 for the young Welshman at the age of 18 before he had played a full season for Chester in the Third Division. Liverpool's confidence was justified as he quickly became the most prolific scorer in the Football League. Though not powerfully built, he has courage to match his tremendous acceleration.

S
HILTON
OCRATES
OUNESS

T
IGANA

Z
ICO

PETER SHILTON

An obsessive goalkeeper who won his first England cap in 1970, aged 21, and was still first choice in 1986. His total of international appearances would have been huge but for having to share duties with Ray Clemence for so long. Shilton has tended to play for unfashionable provincial clubs – Leicester, Stoke, Nottingham Forest and Southampton – though he helped Forest to the League championship and two successive European Cups.

SOCRATES

Socrates Brasileiro Sampaio de Sousa Vieira de Oliveira is a footballer as unusual as his name. A qualified doctor who smokes and drinks, Socrates did not join a leading club (Corinthians) until he was 24. Captain of his country by the World Cup finals only four years later in Spain, where he was an outstanding figure, he signed a lucrative contract with Italy's Fiorentina but returned to Brazil before the 1986 finals.

GRAEME SOUNESS

Born in Edinburgh, a tough and inspiring captain in midfield for Liverpool, Sampdoria and Scotland, who eventually made him a regular international after a long gap between 1975 and 1978. Tottenham had him as an apprentice but he ran away after playing just once, as substitute in a UEFA Cup match, and signed up with Middlesbrough. It cost Liverpool £350,000 to acquire him in 1978. He returned to Scotland as player-manager of Glasgow Rangers in 1986.

JEAN TIGANA

French clubs. Born in the West African state of Mali, a former French colony, he was 20 before Lyon rescued him from Toulon and 25 before France selected him. But a move to Bordeaux followed by a marvellous European Championship in 1984. established him as one of Europe's leading midfielders.

Small and frail, Tigana needed plenty of belief in his own abilities to persevere after rejections by several

ZICO

Born Artur Antunes Coimbra on 3 March 1953, Zico was in the Flamengo first team at 16 and had scored more than 600 goals for them in 14 years when the unglamorous Italian club Udinese raised £2.5 million to sign him. Like that of Socrates, his move was not a great success and the ageing duo returned to Brazil and Flamengo. When fully fit, Zico remains a super asset, not least for his dead-ball shooting.

EUROPEAN FOOTBALLER OF THE YEAR

Since 1956 a select number of journalists from all over Europe have taken part in a poll that is organized by the magazine *France Football* to find the European Footballer of the Year.

With the coming of videos and wider television coverage, their task has become easier than in the earliest years, when few soccer writers had the opportunities to watch all the leading players in any one calendar year.

Whatever the difficulties involved, the list reads, as it should, like a directory of modern European greats and even like a guide to the dominant clubs of each era: from Real Madrid through Barcelona and Inter Milan to Manchester United, then Ajax and Bayern Munich to Juventus – or, perhaps, to Michel Platini, who in 1985 achieved a third successive win. Only Cruyff had previously won three titles, but in his case they were split by a fourth place given

him in 1972. Franz Beckenbauer has the longest span of placings in the top three, between the World Cup year of 1966 and the European championship a decade later.

Not surprisingly, a good World Cup can win a player many votes: Raymond Kopa in 1958, Josef Masopust in 1962, Bobby Charlton in 1966, Gerd Müller in 1970, Johan Cruyff in 1974 and Paolo Rossi in 1982. The notable exception was Kevin Keegan, a

winner in 1978, his first full year with Hamburg, even though England did not play in the Argentina finals.

1956
1 Stanley Matthews (Blackpool and England)
2 Alfredo Di Stéfano (Real Madrid and Spain)
3 Raymond Kopa (Reims and France)
1957
1 Alfredo Di Stéfano (Real Madrid and Spain)
2 Billy Wright (Wolverhampton Wanderers and England)
3 Raymond Kopa (Real Madrid and France)
1958
1 Raymond Kopa (Real Madrid and France)
2 Helmut Rahn (Rot-Weiss Essen and West Germany)
3 Just Fontaine (Reims and France)
1959
1 Alfredo Di Stéfano (Real Madrid and Spain)
2 Raymond Kopa (Real Madrid and France)
3 John Charles (Juventus and Wales)
1960
1 Luis Suarez (Barcelona and Spain)
2 Ferenc Puskás (Real Madrid and Spain)
3 Uwe Seeler (Hamburg and West Germany)
1961
1 Omar Sivori (Juventus and Italy)
2 Luis Suarez (Barcelona and Spain)
3 Johnny Haynes (Fulham and England)

1962
1 Josef Masopust (Dukla Prague and Czechoslovakia)
2 Eusebio (Benfica and Portugal)
3 Karl-Heinz Schnellinger (Cologne and West Germany)
1963
1 Lev Yashin (Dynamo Moscow and USSR)
2 Gianni Rivera (AC Milan and Italy)
3 Jimmy Greaves (Tottenham Hotspur and England)
1964
1 Denis Law (Manchester United and Scotland)
2 Luis Suarez (Internazionale and Spain)
3 Amancio Amaro (Real Madrid and Spain)
1965
1 Eusebio (Benfica and Portugal)
2 Giacinto Facchetti (Internazionale and Italy)
3 Luis Suarez (Internazionale and Spain)
1966
1 Bobby Charlton (Manchester United and England)
2 Eusebio (Benfica and Portugal)
3 Franz Beckenbauer (Bayern Munich and West Germany)

Far left *Alfredo Di Stéfano (Real Madrid) in European Cup action against Barcelona in November 1960. He was Footballer of the Year 1957 and 1959 and runner-up in 1956.*
Near left *Johan Cruyff (Ajax Amsterdam), the first player to win three Footballer of the Year awards (1971, 1973, 1974).*

1967
1 Florian Albert (Ferencváros and Hungary)
2 Bobby Charlton (Manchester United and England)
3 Jimmy Johnstone (Glasgow Celtic and Scotland)
1968
1 George Best (Manchester United and Northern Ireland)
2 Bobby Charlton (Manchester United and England)
3 Dragan Dzajic (Partizan Belgrade and Yugoslavia)
1969
1 Gianni Rivera (AC Milan and Italy)
2 Luigi (Gigi) Riva (Cagliari and Italy)
3 Gerd Müller (Bayern Munich and West Germany)
1970
1 Gerd Müller (Bayern Munich and West Germany)
2 Bobby Moore (West Ham and England)
3 Luigi (Gigi) Riva (Cagliari and Italy)
1971
1 Johan Cruyff (Ajax and Holland)
2 Sandro Mazzola (Internazionale and Italy)
3 George Best (Manchester United and Northern Ireland)
1972
1 Franz Beckenbauer (Bayern Munich and West Germany)
2 Gerd Müller (Bayern Munich and West Germany)
3 Günter Netzer (Borussia Mönchengladbach and West Germany)
1973
1 Johan Cruyff (Barcelona and Holland)
2 Dino Zoff (Juventus and Italy)
3 Gerd Müller (Bayern Munich and West Germany)
1974
1 Johan Cruyff (Barcelona and Holland)
2 Franz Beckenbauer (Bayern Munich and West Germany)
3 Kazimierz Deyna (Legia and Poland)
1975
1 Oleg Blokhin (Dynamo Kiev and USSR)
2 Franz Beckenbauer (Bayern Munich and West Germany)
3 Johan Cruyff (Barcelona and Holland)

1976
1 Franz Beckenbauer (Bayern Munich and West Germany)
2 Rob Rensenbrink (Anderlecht and Holland)
3 Ivo Viktor (Dukla Prague and Czechoslovakia)
1977
1 Allan Simonsen (Borussia Mönchengladbach and Denmark)
2 Kevin Keegan (Hamburg and England)
3 Michel Platini (Nantes and France)
1978
1 Kevin Keegan (Hamburg and England)
2 Hans Krankl (Rapid Vienna and Austria)
3 Rob Rensenbrink (Anderlecht and Holland)
1979
1 Kevin Keegan (Hamburg and England)
2 Karl-Heinz Rummenigge (Bayern Munich and West Germany)
3 Ruud Krol (Ajax and Holland)
1980
1 Karl-Heinz Rummenigge (Bayern Munich and West Germany)
2 Bernd Schuster (Barcelona and West Germany)
3 Michel Platini (St-Etienne and France)
1981
1 Karl-Heinz Rummenigge (Bayern Munich and West Germany)
2 Paul Breitner (Bayern Munich and West Germany)
3 Bernd Schuster (Barcelona and West Germany)
1982
1 Paolo Rossi (Juventus and Italy)
2 Alain Giresse (Bordeaux and France)
3 Zbigniew Boniek (Juventus and Poland)
1983
1 Michel Platini (Juventus and France)
2 Kenny Dalglish (Liverpool and Scotland)
3 Allan Simonsen (Vejle and Denmark)
1984
1 Michel Platini (Juventus and France)
2 Jean Tigana (Bordeaux and France)
3 Preben Elkjær-Larsen (Verona and Denmark)
1985
1 Michel Platini (Juventus and France)
2 Preben Elkjær-Larsen (Verona and Denmark)
3 Bernd Schuster (Barcelona and West Germany)

Near right *Karl-Heinz Rummenigge (here in Internazionale colours) won his two titles (1980, 1981) when with Bayern Munich; he was also runner-up (to Kevin Keegan) in 1979.* **Far right** *Michel Platini (Juventus), the greatest European player of the early 1980s, is the only footballer to have won three titles in succession (1983–5).*

STANLEY MATTHEWS · MICHEL PLATINI

THE EUROPEAN CUP

*L*ike so many other international football competitions, the European Cup was the brainchild of a Frenchman. Gabriel Hanot, football journalist on *L'Equipe*, was the moving force behind the first tournament in which 16 invited teams took part. The competition had been prompted in part by English claims that Wolverhampton Wanderers, having beaten Honvéd of Hungary in December 1954 (on a specially watered pitch which sapped the Hungarians' stamina) was the world's top club.

In fact, for the first two seasons English officials refused permission to the Football League champions to take part and it was Spain, Italy and France who dominated the first competitions. Real Madrid's magnificent team won the European Cup for the first five seasons, culminating in a stunning display against Eintracht Frankfurt in 1960. Benfica and the two Milan clubs took over, without their ever approaching the standards set by Alfredo Di Stéfano and his Real team mates.

There were memorable victories from Scotland's Glasgow Celtic and England's Manchester United; then hat tricks by the gifted Ajax and Bayern Munich teams, followed by a more prosaic but nevertheless

Defenders Alan Kennedy (left) and Phil Neal celebrate after Liverpool's dour victory over Real Madrid in the 1981 European Cup final in Paris. Kennedy scored the only goal of the match.

remarkable run of six wins for English clubs (five of them by one goal to nil). However, immediate prospects of the English adding to their tally disappeared with UEFA's ban on their clubs following the riot at the 1985 final in Brussels in which 39 spectators died.

Results of finals:
1956 (Paris) Real Madrid (Spain) v. Reims (France) 4–3
1957 (Madrid) Real Madrid (Spain) v. Fiorentina (Italy) 2–0
1958 (Brussels) Real Madrid (Spain) v. AC Milan (Italy) 3–2 after extra time
1959 (Stuttgart) Real Madrid (Spain) v. Reims (France) 2–0
1960 (Glasgow) Real Madrid (Spain) v. Eintracht Frankfurt (West Germany) 7–3
1961 (Berne) Benfica (Portugal) v. Barcelona (Spain) 3–2
1962 (Amsterdam) Benfica (Portugal) v. Real Madrid (Spain) 5–3
1963 (Wembley) AC Milan (Italy) v. Benfica (Portugal) 2–1
1964 (Vienna) Internazionale (Italy) v. Real Madrid (Spain) 3–1
1965 (Milan) Internazionale (Italy) v. Benfica (Portugal) 1–0
1966 (Brussels) Real Madrid (Spain) v. Partizan (Yugoslavia) 2–1
1967 (Lisbon) Glasgow Celtic (Scotland) v. Internazionale (Italy) 2–1
1968 (Wembley) Manchester United (England) v. Benfica (Portugal) 4–1 after extra time
1969 (Madrid) AC Milan (Italy) v. Ajax (Holland) 4–1
1970 (Milan) Feyenoord (Holland) v. Glasgow Celtic (Scotland) 2–1 after extra time
1971 (Wembley) Ajax (Holland) v. Panathinaikos (Greece) 2–0
1972 (Rotterdam) Ajax (Holland) v. Internazionale (Italy) 2–0
1973 (Belgrade) Ajax (Holland) v. Juventus (Italy) 1–0
1974 (Brussels) Bayern Munich (West Germany) v. Atlético Madrid (Spain) 4–0 after 1–1 draw
1975 (Paris) Bayern Munich (West Germany) v. Leeds United (England) 2–0
1976 (Glasgow) Bayern Munich (West Germany) v. St-Etienne (France) 1–0
1977 (Rome) Liverpool (England) v. Borussia Mönchengladbach (West Germany) 3–1
1978 (Wembley) Liverpool (England) v. FC Bruges (Belgium) 1–0
1979 (Munich) Nottingham Forest (England) v. Malmö FF (Sweden) 1–0
1980 (Madrid) Nottingham Forest (England) v. Hamburg (West Germany) 1–0
1981 (Paris) Liverpool (England) v. Real Madrid (Spain) 1–0
1982 (Rotterdam) Aston Villa (England) v. Bayern Munich (West Germany) 1–0
1983 (Athens) Hamburg (West Germany) v. Juventus (Italy) 1–0
1984 (Rome) Liverpool (England) v. AS Roma (Italy) 1–1 after extra time: Liverpool won 4–2 on penalties
1985 (Brussels) Juventus (Italy) v. Liverpool (England) 1–0
1986 (Seville) Steaua (Romania) v. Barcelona (Spain) 0–0 after extra time: Steaua won 2–0 on penalties

THE EUROPEAN CUP WINNERS'

Domestic cup football has never been of great importance in many European countries but it is significant that by the mid-1960s, once the Cup Winners' Cup was established, almost all of them had a regular competition.

The first tournament in 1961 involved just ten clubs and the organizers were not confident enough of a high level of support to stage the final in a neutral country. However, clubs like Fiorentina, Glasgow Rangers, Atlético Madrid and Tottenham Hotspur provided a good standard of football and only for that first season was the final played over two legs.

Although Spain, Italy, West Germany and Britain have tended to dominate, their monopoly has not remained as generally unchallenged as in the European Cup: in 1975 a major European final was contested by two Eastern European teams for the first time when Dynamo Kiev of Russia defeated Ferencváros of Hungary.

With an increasing variety of teams competing, only a select few have won the Cup Winners' Cup twice.

Results of finals:
1961 (two legs) Fiorentina (Italy) v. Glasgow Rangers (Scotland) 2–0, 2–1 (4–1)
1962 (Stuttgart) Atlético Madrid (Spain) v. Fiorentina (Italy) 3–0 after 1–1 draw in Glasgow
1963 (Rotterdam) Tottenham Hotspur (England) v. Atlético Madrid (Spain) 5–1
1964 (Antwerp) Sporting Lisbon (Portugal) v. MTK Budapest (Hungary) 1–0 after 3–3 draw in Brussels
1965 (Wembley) West Ham (England) v. 1860 Munich (West Germany) 2–0
1966 (Glasgow) Borussia Dortmund (West Germany) v. Liverpool (England) 2–1 after extra time
1967 (Nuremberg) Bayern Munich (West Germany) v. Glasgow Rangers (Scotland) 1–0 after extra time
1968 (Rotterdam) AC Milan (Italy) v. Hamburg (West Germany) 2–0
1969 (Basle) Slovan Bratislava (Czechoslovakia) v. Barcelona (Spain) 3–2
1970 (Vienna) Manchester City (England) v. Górnik Zabrze (Poland) 2–1
1971 (Athens) Chelsea (England) v. Real Madrid (Spain) 2–1 after 1–1 draw
1972 (Barcelona) Glasgow Rangers (Scotland) v. Dynamo Moscow (USSR) 3–2
1973 (Salonika) AC Milan (Italy) v. Leeds United (England) 1–0
1974 (Rotterdam) Magdeburg (East Germany) v. AC Milan (Italy) 2–0
1975 (Basle) Dynamo Kiev (USSR) v. Ferencváros (Hungary) 3–0
1976 (Brussels) Anderlecht (Belgium) v. West Ham (England) 4–2
1977 (Amsterdam) Hamburg (West Germany) v. Anderlecht (Belgium) 2–0
1978 (Paris) Anderlecht (Belgium) v. FK Austria (Austria) 4–0
1979 (Basle) Barcelona (Spain) v. Fortuna Düsseldorf (West Germany) 4–3 after extra time
1980 (Brussels) Valencia (Spain) v. Arsenal (England) 0–0 after extra time: Valencia won 4–3 on penalties
1981 (Düsseldorf) Dynamo Tbilisi (USSR) v. Carl Zeiss Jena (East Germany) 2–1
1982 (Barcelona) Barcelona (Spain) v. Standard Liège (Belgium) 2–1
1983 (Gothenburg) Aberdeen (Scotland) v. Real Madrid (Spain) 2–1 after extra time
1984 (Basle) Juventus (Italy) v. Porto (Portugal) 2–1
1985 (Rotterdam) Everton (England) v. Rapid Vienna (Austria) 3–1
1986 (Lyon) Dynamo Kiev (USSR) v. Atlético Madrid (Spain) 3–0

The Barcelona side that won the 1982 Cup Winners' Cup final (in their own stadium!) against Standard Liège of Belgium.

THE INTER-CITIES FAIRS' CUP/ UEFA CUP

*T*he UEFA Cup, now attracting 64 teams each season, including all the best clubs not actually winning their national league title, had obscure origins. Between 1955 and 1958 ten clubs and representative elevens played four groups, a semifinal and final, all of which were supposed to coincide with a trade fair in their locality.

It took two years to complete the next tournament, before the competition was standardized to the pattern of the two other big European competitions: the only exception was that the final has always been played on a home-and-away basis, except for the 1964 and 1965 experiment.

There was a change in 1971 when UEFA (the Union of European Football Associations, the governing body of European football) gave the competition its own name in place of the previous title. Barcelona, the club that had won the first final in 1958, beat Leeds United, who took the 1971 title, for the right to keep the Fairs' trophy. The change of name did not interrupt a winning sequence of six years (1968–73) by English clubs.

Anderlecht's Grun fails to stop Spurs' Archibald in the 1984 UEFA Cup final. Spurs won on penalties after two 1–1 draws.

Results of finals:
As Fairs' Cup
1958 Barcelona (Spain) v. London XI (England) 2–2, 6–0 (8–2)
1960 Barcelona (Spain) v. Birmingham City (England) 0–0, 4–1 (4–1)
1961 AS Roma (Italy) v. Birmingham City (England) 2–2, 2–0 (4–2)
1962 Valencia (Spain) v. Barcelona (Spain) 6–2, 1–1 (7–3)
1963 Valencia (Spain) v. Dynamo Zagreb (Yugoslavia) 2–1, 2–0 (4–1)
1964 Real Zaragoza (Spain) v. Valencia (Spain) 2–1 in Barcelona
1965 Ferencváros (Hungary) v. Juventus (Italy) 1–0 in Turin
1966 Barcelona (Spain) v. Real Zaragoza (Spain) 0–1, 4–2 after extra time (4–3)
1967 Dynamo Zagreb (Yugoslavia) v. Leeds United (England) 2–0, 0–0 (2–0)
1968 Leeds United (England) v. Ferencváros (Hungary) 1–0, 0–0 (1–0)
1969 Newcastle (England) v. Ujpesti Dózsa (Hungary) 3–0, 3–2 (6–2)
1970 Arsenal (England) v. Anderlecht (Belgium) 1–3, 3–0 (4–3)
1971 Leeds United (England) v. Juventus (Italy) 2–2, 1–1 after extra time (3–3: Leeds won on away goals)
As UEFA Cup
1972 Tottenham Hotspur (England) v. Wolves (England) 2–1, 1–1 (3–2)
1973 Liverpool (England) v. Borussia Mönchengladbach (West Germany) 3–0, 0–2, (3–2)
1974 Feyenoord (Holland) v. Tottenham Hotspur (England) 2–2, 2–0 (4–2)
1975 Borussia Mönchengladbach (West Germany) v. Twente Enschede (Holland) 0–0, 5–1 (5–1)
1976 Liverpool (England) v. FC Bruges (Belgium) 3–2, 1–1 (4–3)
1977 Juventus (Italy) v. Athletic Bilbao (Spain) 1–0, 1–2, (2–2: Juventus won on away goal)
1978 PSV Eindhoven (Holland) v. Bastia (France) 0–0, 3–0 (3–0)
1979 Borussia Mönchengladbach (West Germany) v. Red Star Belgrade 1–1, 1–0 (2–1)
1980 Eintracht Frankfurt (West Germany) v. Borussia Mönchengladbach (West Germany) 2–3, 1–0 (3–3: Eintracht won on away goals)
1981 Ipswich (England) v. AZ 67 Alkmaar (Holland) 3–0, 2–4, (5–4)
1982 IFK Gothenburg (Sweden) v. Hamburg (West Germany) 1–0, 3–0 (4–0)
1983 Anderlecht (Belgium) v. Benfica (Portugal) 1–0, 1–1 (2–1)
1984 Tottenham Hotspur (England) v. Anderlecht (Belgium) 1–1, 1–1 after extra time (2–2: Tottenham won 4–3 on penalties)
1985 Real Madrid (Spain) v. Videoton (Hungary) 3–0, 0–1 (3–1)
1986 Real Madrid (Spain) v. Cologne (West Germany) 5–1, 0–2 (5–3)

SOUTH AMERICAN CLUB CHAMPIONSHIP

*F*eatures of the South American Club Championship (or *Copa Libertadoros*) have been the successes of Argentinian, as opposed to Brazilian, clubs; the number of tightly contested finals requiring a play-off in a neutral country; and, as the tournament became more lucrative and prestigious, the number of violent games.

After the early victories of Peñarol and Santos, Argentinian teams reached the final for 16 successive years, winning 12 times, and not until the 1980s were Brazilian clubs regularly represented.

Apart from Uruguay (with great rivals Peñarol and Nacional), only Paraguay has broken the domination of the big two, when Olimpia took the title in 1979.

Results of finals:
1960 Peñarol (Uruguay) v. Olimpia (Paraguay) 1–0, 1–1
1961 Peñarol (Uruguay) v. Palmeiras (Brazil) 1–0, 1–1
1962 Santos (Brazil) v. Peñarol (Uruguay) 2–1, 2–3, 3–0
1963 Santos (Brazil) v. Boca Juniors (Argentina) 3–2, 2–1
1964 Independiente (Argentina) v. Nacional (Uruguay) 0–0, 1–0
1965 Independiente (Argentina) v. Peñarol (Uruguay) 1–0, 1–3, 4–1
1966 Peñarol (Uruguay) v. River Plate (Argentina) 2–0, 2–3, 4–2 after extra time
1967 Racing Club (Argentina) v. Nacional (Uruguay) 0–0, 0–0, 2–1
1968 Estudiantes (Argentina) v. Palmeiras (Brazil) 2–1, 1–3, 2–0
1969 Estudiantes (Argentina) v. Nacional (Uruguay) 1–0, 2–0
1970 Estudiantes (Argentina) v. Peñarol (Uruguay) 1–0, 0–0
1971 Nacional (Uruguay) v. Estudiantes (Argentina) 0–1, 1–0, 2–0
1972 Independiente (Argentina) v. Universitario (Peru) 0–0, 2–1
1973 Independiente (Argentina) v. Colo Colo (Chile) 1–1, 0–0, 2–1
1974 Independiente (Argentina) v. São Paulo (Brazil) 1–2, 2–0, 1–0
1975 Independiente (Argentina) v. Unión Española (Chile) 0–1, 3–1, 2–0
1976 Cruzeiro (Brazil) v. River Plate (Argentina) 4–1, 1–2, 3–2
1977 Boca Juniors (Argentina) v. Cruzeiro (Brazil) 1–0, 0–1, 0–0 after extra time (Boca won 5–4 on penalties)
1978 Boca Juniors (Argentina) v. Deportivo Cali (Columbia) 0–0, 4–0
1979 Olimpia (Paraguay) v. Boca Juniors (Argentina) 2–0, 0–0
1980 Nacional (Uruguay) v. Internacional (Brazil) 0–0, 1–0
1981 Flamengo (Brazil) v. Cobreola (Chile) 2–1, 0–1, 2–0
1982 Peñarol (Uruguay) v. Cobreola (Chile) 0–0, 1–0
1983 Gremio (Brazil) v. Peñarol (Uruguay) 1–1, 2–1
1984 Independiente (Argentina) v. Gremio (Brazil) 1–0, 0–0
1985 Argentinos Juniors (Argentina) v. America (Colombia) 1–0, 0–1, 1–1 (Argentinos won 5–4 on penalties)

WORLD CUP FOR CLUBS

*O*nce the South American championship started, it was an obvious development for the winners to play the European Cup holders for the unofficial title of world champion club.

Sadly, many of the games were scarred by violence – notably Santos against AC Milan in 1963 and those where British clubs met Argentinian sides a few years later. The lure of the Japanese yen, though, revived a devalued competition. It is now played as a single match in Tokyo; disruption to competing clubs is compensated for in handsome prize money.

Results:
1960 Real Madrid (Spain) v. Peñarol (Uruguay) 0–0, 5–1
1961 Peñarol (Uruguay) v. Benfica (Portugal) 0–1, 5–0, 2–1
1962 Santos (Brazil) v. Benfica (Portugal) 3–2, 5–2
1963 Santos (Brazil) v. AC Milan (Italy) 2–4, 4–2, 1–0
1964 Internazionale (Italy) v. Independiente (Argentina) 0–1, 2–0, 1–0 after extra time
1965 Internazionale (Italy) v. Independiente (Argentina) 3–0, 0–0
1966 Peñarol (Uruguay) v. Real Madrid (Spain) 2–0, 2–0
1967 Racing Club (Argentina) v. Glasgow Celtic (Scotland) 0–1, 2–1, 1–0
1968 Estudiantes (Argentina) v. Manchester United (England) 1–0, 1–1
1969 AC Milan (Italy) v. Estudiantes (Argentina) 3–0, 1–2
1970 Feyenoord (Holland) v. Estudiantes (Argentina) 2–2, 1–0
1971 Nacional (Uruguay) v. Panathinaikos (Greece) 1–1, 2–1
1972 Ajax (Holland) v. Independiente (Argentina) 0–1, 3–0
1973 Independiente (Argentina) v. Juventus (Italy) 1–0 (in Rome)
1974 Atlético Madrid (Spain) v. Independiente (Argentina) 0–1, 2–0
1976 Bayern Munich (West Germany) v. Cruzeiro (Brazil) 2–0, 0–0
1977 Boca Juniors (Argentina) v. Borussia Mönchengladbach (West Germany) 2–2, 3–0
1979 Olimpia (Paraguay) v. Malmö FF (Sweden) 1–0, 2–1
1980 Nacional (Uruguay) v. Nottingham Forest (England) 1–0
1981 Flamengo (Brazil) v. Liverpool (England) 3–0
1982 Peñarol (Uruguay) v. Aston Villa (England) 2–0
1983 Gremio (Brazil) v. Hamburg (West Germany) 2–1 after extra time
1984 Independiente (Argentina) v. Liverpool (England) 1–0
1985 Juventus (Italy) v. Argentinos Juniors (Argentina) 2–2 after extra time (Juventus won 4–2 on penalties)
Note: Play-offs were necessary in 1961 (Montevideo), 1963 (Rio de Janeiro), 1964 (Madrid), and 1967 (Montevideo). No competition in 1975 and 1978. All matches from 1980 onwards played in Tokyo.

THE EUROPEAN CHAMPIONSHIP

1960
Host: France
Winner: USSR

Only 17 countries entered the first competition for the Henri Delauney Cup, played on a two-leg knockout basis until the semifinal. France, even without Kopa and Fontaine, had much the most entertaining team, scoring 21 goals in five games, but Paris was denied the chance of a home victory by defeat in a high-scoring semifinal.
Semifinals:
USSR 3 Czechoslovakia 0
France 4 Yugoslavia 5
Final:
USSR 2 (Metreveli, Ponedelnik)
Yugoslavia 1 (Netto own goal)
(after extra time) 18,000

1964
Host: Spain
Winner: Spain

Twenty-nine countries, almost a full complement, took part this time. A lop-sided draw helped Denmark reach the last four, but World Cup finalists Czechoslovakia went out in the first round, like England (beaten 5–2 by France, who subsequently lost home and away to Hungary). Spain made the most of good fortune and home advantage with late winning goals in its last two matches.
Semifinals:
Spain 2 Hungary 1
USSR 3 Denmark 0
Final:
Spain 2 (Pereda, Marcelino)
USSR 1 (Khusainov) 120,000

1968
Host: Italy
Winner: Italy

There was a sensation when West Germany could only draw a qualifying match in Albania, allowing Yugoslavia to qualify from its group. The Yugoslavs went on to defeat France, then the World Cup holders England, before unluckily going down to the host country.
Semifinals:
Italy 0 USSR 0
(Italy won on toss of a coin)
Yugoslavia 1 England 0
Final:
Italy 1 (Domenghini)
Yugoslavia 1 (Dzajic) 75,000
Italy 2 (Riva, Anastasi)
Yugoslavia 0 60,000

1972
Host: Belgium
Winner: West Germany

The West Germans stood head and shoulders above the rest with Maier, Beckenbauer, Breitner, Netzer and Müller all outstanding. Host country Belgium pushed the Germans closest, but was undone by Gerd Müller, whose two goals in the final took him past a half century in only 41 matches!
Semifinals:
West Germany 2 Belgium 1
USSR 1 Hungary 0
Final:
West Germany 3 (Müller 2, Wimmer)
USSR 0 43,437

Gerd Müller (jumping) is congratulated by his skipper Franz Beckenbauer after scoring West Germany's first goal in the 1972 European Championship final.

7

French midfielders Tigana (extreme left) and Platini flank Spain's Francisco during the 1984 final in Paris.

1976
Host: Yugoslavia
Winner:
Czechoslovakia

A repeat of the 1974 World Cup final seemed the most likely outcome. After a wonderful series of matches, however, West Germany was denied another triumph on penalty kicks – Czechoslovakia won the competition almost two years after beginning it with a 3–0 defeat by England at Wembley.

Semifinals:
Czechoslovakia 3
Holland 1 (after extra time)
West Germany 4
Yugoslavia 2 (after extra time)
Final:
Czechoslovakia 2 (Svehlik, Dobias)
West Germany 2 (Müller, Hölzenbein)
(after extra time: Czechoslovakia won on penalties)   45,000

1980
Host: Italy
Winner:
West Germany

The complete antithesis of 1976, a tedious tournament of eight teams in which West Germany's 3–2 win over Holland was the only high point. Belgium unexpectedly finished above Italy and England in its group, but was beaten in the final by Horst Hrübesch's header.
Semifinals:
none (Czechoslovakia and Italy were runners-up in groups)
Final:
West Germany 2 (Hrübesch 2)
Belgium 1 (Van der Eycken)   47,864

1984
Host: France
Winner: France

Michel Platini was at his most devastating with at least one goal in every one of France's matches, although Yugoslavia and Portugal pushed the French hard. Denmark would have been popular finalists, but lost out on penalties to Spain.

Semifinals:
France 3 Portugal 2 (after extra time)
Spain 1 Denmark 1 (after extra time: Spain won on penalties)
Final:
France 2 (Platini, Bellone)
Spain 0   80,000

THE SOUTH AMERICAN CHAMPIONSHIP

Winners:
1916 Uruguay
1917 Uruguay
1919 Brazil
1920 Uruguay
1921 Argentina
1922 Brazil
1923 Uruguay
1924 Uruguay
1925 Argentina
1926 Uruguay
1927 Argentina
1929 Argentina
1935 Uruguay
1937 Argentina
1939 Peru

1941* Argentina
1942 Uruguay
1945* Argentina
1946* Argentina
1947 Argentina
1949 Brazil
1953 Paraguay
1955 Argentina
1956* Uruguay
1957 Argentina
1959 Argentina
1959* Uruguay
1963 Bolivia
1967 Uruguay
1975 Peru
1979 Paraguay

1983 Uruguay

*Unofficial

1930

Host: Uruguay
Winner: Uruguay

By the late 1920s professionalism was increasingly in evidence and the Olympic Games no longer automatically included the world's best players and teams. FIFA (Fédération Internationale de Football Association), which had been founded in 1904, decided that the first World Cup competition for the Jules Rimet Trophy should be hosted by Uruguay, the Olympic champions – then found that only four European countries (France, Belgium, Romania and Yugoslavia) were prepared to make the long journey to Montevideo.

Uruguay, Argentina,

Jules Rimet (left) presents his World Cup trophy to the president of the Uruguay FA after the 1930 final.

Brazil and the United States were seeded to head the four groups and only the Brazilians failed to win theirs. The Yugoslavs beat them but, like the USA, were crushed 6–1 in their semifinal.

So the expected final, a repeat of the 1928 Olympics, came about. Although Argentina led 2–1 at half-time, the host country set a pattern for the future by taking victory in the end in front of a wildly enthusiastic crowd of 90,000.

Semifinals:
Argentina 6 USA 1
Uruguay 6
Yugoslavia 1
Final:
Uruguay 4 (Dorado, Cea, Iriarte, Castro)
Argentina 2 (Peucelle, Stabile)   90,000

1934

Host: Italy
Winner: Italy

The World Cup was catching on! Thirty-two countries entered, but not Uruguay. Upset by the lukewarm European response four years earlier and a domestic soccer strike, the Uruguayans stayed at home, leaving Vittorio Pozzo's Italy and Hugo Meisl's Austria as favourites.

The Austrians eliminated France, after extra time. The Italians came through against Spain, who they had to play twice in two days, to meet Austria in the semifinal and powered

Italy's players carry their team manager Vittorio Pozzo in triumph after beating Czechoslovakia in the 1934 final.

through the Milanese mud for a 1–0 win.

The talented Czechs were their opponents in the final and went ahead 20 minutes from time. But Raimondo Orsi equalized and in

extra time a weary Angelo Schiavio managed to shoot past the Czech goalkeeper and captain Planicka. The host country had won again.

Semifinals:
Czechoslovakia 3
Germany 1
Italy 1 Austria 0
Final:
Italy 2 (Orsi, Schiavio)
Czechoslovakia 1 (Puc)
(after extra time) 50,000

1938

Host: France
Winner: Italy

With a world war only 15 months away, political considerations were already casting a shadow over football pitches. Spain was in the middle of a civil war and the fine Austrian team had to withdraw from the competition when Hitler annexed that country. England declined to compete as replacement, leaving 15 qualifiers (from an entry of 36) who again played a straight knockout competition.

There were some fascinating first-round matches. Italy had a narrow escape against the unconsidered amateurs of Norway; poor Ernest Willimowski of Poland scored four times, only to finish on the losing side against Brazil (5–6); Cuba beat Romania; and Germany, buoyed up by Austrian players, lost to Switzerland.

The French, having beaten Belgium, unfortunately found themselves up against the holders and lost 3–1, the Italians going on to retain their trophy by defeating Brazil and then Hungary.

Pozzo holds the Jules Rimet trophy aloft after his team had made it two World Cup wins in a row.

Semifinals:
Italy 2 Brazil 1
Hungary 5 Sweden 1
Final:
Italy 4 (Colaussi 2,
Piola 2)
Hungary 2 (Titkos,
Sarossi)   45,000

1950

Host: Brazil
Winner: Uruguay

Another depleted competition which produced a dramatic climax. The four British countries had belatedly joined in and had even been favoured with a qualifying group of their own, ensuring two qualifiers. But the Scots, having insisted they would only compete if they won the group, could only finish second to England. Argentina, Austria, France, Hungary and Portugal all declined to compete, and a partitioned Germany had not resumed international fixtures.

All this left just 13 qualifiers and 4 oddly assorted groups. Uruguay had to play only Bolivia and duly won 8–0 to reach the last four. England and Italy were seeded to join the Uruguayans but both failed: England lost to both Spain and the USA (the country's most embarrassing international defeat ever). Italy, whose team had been decimated by the Superga air disaster of 1949, was edged out by Sweden.

Semifinals and a final were eschewed in favour of another group, or pool, in which the Brazilians brushed aside Sweden (7–1) and Spain (6–1), thus needing only a draw from their last match against Uruguay in Rio de Janeiro. A world record 200,000 crowd thronged the Maracaná stadium for what was the finale, if not strictly speaking the final. The home majority was stunned as Uruguay came from behind to win back the Cup after 20 years.

Brazil's winger Friaça sends a bullet-fast header over the bar in the final match of 1950. Inspired by centre-half Varela and inside-left Schiaffino, Uruguay won 2–1.

Group winners: Brazil, Spain, Sweden, Uruguay
Final match: Uruguay 2 (Schiaffino, Ghiggia)
Brazil 1 (Friaça) 200,000

8

1954

West Germany's Max Morlock beats Hungary's keeper Grosics in the 1954 final. The Hungarians, hottest favourites in World Cup history, were disrupted by an injury to their captain and chief marksman, Ferenc Puskás.

Host: Switzerland
Winner:
    West Germany

For once the host country clearly had no chance of winning: Switzerland was not even seeded to reach the quarter-final, though the side did so by virtue of a 4–1 play-off victory against Italy.

The Hungarians were understandably the hottest favourites yet. Just before the 1950 finals, they lost a friendly to Austria – then began an unbeaten run that took them right through to the 1954 competition!

Theirs was a magnificent side, of József Bozsik, Nándor Hidegkuti, Sándor Kocsis and Ferenc Puskás. Even with Puskás injured (in a group match against the West Germans) they swept to the final by scoring 25 goals in 4 games.

Brazil lost to Hungary at the quarter-final stage, the infamous Battle of Berne in which there were three sendings-off and brawling in the dressing room. Austria, its greatest years behind it, beat Switzerland 7–5, Uruguay put out England and West Germany beat Yugoslavia: then ditched Austria 6–1 in the semifinal.

So to the final in Berne: Hungary against West Germany for the second time in the tournament. The West Germans, who had lost the first game 8–3, must have wondered about a repeat when they went two down in eight minutes; but Max Morlock and Helmut Rahn equalized and with only five minutes left Rahn slid home what turned out to be the winning goal. West Germany, seeded even below Turkey in its group, had completed the most astounding World Cup win yet.

Semifinals:
Hungary 4 Uruguay 2
West Germany 6
Austria 1
Final:
West Germany 3 (Rahn 2, Morlock)
Hungary 2 (Puskás, Czibor)   60,000

1958

Brazil's brilliant team parades the national flag after beating Sweden in the 1958 final. 'Little Bird' Garrincha is at centre-right.

Host: Sweden
Winner: Brazil

Brazil's stylish 4–2–4 system signalled a new era and a new order. Hungary, sadly, was no longer a force after the 1956 revolution; neither were the Austrians or Italians; and England's hopes were dimmed by the Manchester United air crash at Munich.

All four British countries qualified and Northern Ireland and Wales both played gallantly to reach the quarter-final. The Brazilians beat the Welsh and were into the semifinal without conceding a goal. They swept through 5–2 against an exciting French side, which after failing to win any of its six matches immediately before the tournament found inspiration from Raymond Kopa and Just Fontaine. Third place after scoring 23 goals in six matches was a deserved reward.

The West Germans, though their side was much changed from 1954, still had Helmut Rahn to score goals, but Sweden, now benefiting from the host country's traditional massive support, got the better of them to reach the final.

Although the Swedes scored first there, through Nils Liedholm, the Brazilians, with Garrincha and the 17-year-old Pelé outstanding, asserted their undeniable superiority to claim their first World Cup.

Semifinals:
Brazil 5 France 2
Sweden 3
West Germany 1
Final:
Brazil 5 (Vavà 2, Pelé 2, Zagalo)
Sweden 2 (Liedholm, Simonsson)   49,737

1962

Zito jumps for joy after scoring Brazil's second goal against the resourceful Czechs in the 1962 final. In Pelé's absence through injury, Garrincha's dribbling and ferocious shooting inspired Brazil through the earlier rounds.

Host: Chile
Winner: Brazil

A competition comprising much dreary and dirty football redeemed only by Brazil, and Garrincha in particular. *Catenaccio*, the defensive play all the rage in Italy, was also employed by Spain under Helenio Herrera of Inter Milan. Neither progressed beyond their group, Italy losing to the host country after two of its men had been sent off.

Brazil won its group with two narrow victories and a goalless draw against the Czechs, not looking as good as the team of 1958. Pelé, injured in the Brazilians' second match, played no further part. In the quarterfinal Brazil met England, who despite the presence of Johnny Haynes, Bobby Charlton and Jimmy Greaves, plus a young Bobby Moore, only scraped through its group and now lost 3–1 under much torment from Garrincha.

Chile unexpectedly beat the Soviet Union but fell to Brazil in the semifinal, where Garrincha was one of two players sent off. Czechoslovakia defeated Hungary, and then Yugoslavia (who had put out West Germany) to make the final and meet Brazil again. The Czechs took the lead through their imperious captain Josef Masopust, but Pelé's replacement Amarildo equalized and made a second for Zito. Vavà, one of eight survivors from 1958, scored another near the end.

Semifinals:
Brazil 4 Chile 2
Czechoslovakia 3
Yugoslavia 1
Final:
Brazil 3
(Amarildo, Zito, Vavà)
Czechoslovakia 1
(Masopust)   68,679

1966

England's 1966 heroes: from left, Stiles and Jack Charlton, Banks, Ball, Peters, Hurst, Moore (with cup), Wilson, Cohen, Bobby Charlton. Missing is striker Hunt.

Host: England
Winner: England

The Brazilians, attempting to win for a record third successive tournament, did not even reach the quarter-final; they received some nasty treatment from Portugal and Bulgaria, and shared in a magnificent match against Hungary who beat them 3–1.

Only the North Koreans, of all people, threatened the European monopoly. Having beaten Italy 1–0 with Pak Doo Ik's goal, they led Portugal 3–0 after 24 minutes of their quarter-final! Then Eusebio took a hand, scoring four and making a fifth to earn a place in the all-European semifinals.

Like most host countries, England had to withstand accusations of favouritism. The English won their group comfortably but did not break down Argentina in the quarter-final until Antonio Rattin was sent off. Portugal proved equally difficult opponents, going down 2–1 at Wembley – where England played every match.

West Germany, underrated as in 1954, scored first in the final and will claim for evermore that England's decisive third goal should not have been awarded. A linesman decided the ball had crossed the line and when Geoff Hurst scored again in the last minute of extra time he became the first player to achieve a hat trick in the World Cup final.

Semifinals:
England 2 Portugal 1
West Germany 2 USSR 1
Final:
England 4 (Hurst 3, Peters)
West Germany 2 (Haller, Weber)
(after extra time) 93,802

1970

Brazil's victorious 1970 side. With midfield inspiration from Gerson and Rivelino, an attack spearheaded by Tostão and Jairzinho, and Pelé's genius pervading almost every creative thrust, Brazil played the most exhilarating football yet seen in a World Cup final.

Host: Mexico
Winner: Brazil

The English went to Mexico regarding Brazil and West Germany as the teams most likely to take their trophy – and soon found themselves playing both. Defeat by Brazil in a closely contested group match meant they would meet the West Germans in their quarter-final. It was an epic match, played in the steaming heat of León in which England, without goalkeeper Gordon Banks, led 2–0 only to lose to goals by Franz Beckenbauer, Uwe Seeler and, in extra time, Gerd Müller.

Extra time faced the West Germans, too, in their semifinal against Italy. This time Beckenbauer had to play through it with his arm strapped to his side after a cynical foul. Goals by Luigi Riva and Gianni Rivera edged the Italians home by 4–3.

The Brazilians meanwhile swept everyone aside, South American rivals Peru and Uruguay falling 4–2 and 3–1. They even ended an odd sequence in which the team scoring first in every postwar final had lost. Pelé got that first goal with a typical header and though Roberto Boninsegna equalized, Italy could not withstand an attack consisting of Jairzinho (who scored in every round), Tostão, Pelé and Rivelino.

Semifinals:
Brazil 3 Uruguay 1
Italy 4 West Germany 3
(after extra time)
Final:
Brazil 4 (Pelé, Gerson, Jairzinho, Alberto)
Italy 1
(Boninsegna)   107,412

1974

1974 World Cup final: Holland's captain Cruyff (left) and West German keeper Maier register pain, while German skipper Beckenbauer appears to be counting them out. West German organization prevailed over Dutch flair in this clash between the chief proponents of 'total football'.

Host: West Germany
Winner:
    West Germany

Holland and West Germany, able to draw on the dazzling talents of Ajax Amsterdam and Bayern Munich respectively, had to be fancied as the world tournament returned to Europe. Brazil, sadly, decided that the football that had charmed the world in 1970 would not suffice. To be fair, the side had lost outstanding players, including Pelé, but results from the group illustrated their new priorities. Goalless draws against Yugoslavia and Scotland were followed by a 3–0 win over Zaire – just sufficient to qualify ahead of the Scots.

A new system meant further mini-leagues instead of quarter-finals. In group A Johan Cruyff's Holland, easily the most exciting team, beat Argentina, East Germany and then Brazil without conceding a goal – the Dutch scoring eight themselves.

The West Germans should have been in that group instead of their eastern neighbours, but had lost to them and finished second rather than first in the qualifying section. That left them free to beat Yugoslavia, Sweden and impressive Poland to reach the final.

The final had a sensational start, Johan Neeskens converting a penalty before a single German player had touched the ball. Paul Breitner equalized from another penalty and Gerd Müller, *der Bomber*, became the man to win the Cup when he swivelled to shoot past goalkeeper Jan Jongbloed.

Semifinals:
none (Poland and Brazil runners-up in second round groups)
Final:
West Germany 2 (Breitner pen., Müller) Holland 1 (Neeskens pen.) 77,833

1978

Holland's Johnny Rep beats Argentina's skipper Daniel Passarella in the air during the 1978 final. A tense war of attrition for 90 minutes, it was eventually won by Argentina in extra time.

Host: Argentina
Winner: Argentina

Could a European team win in the Americas for the first time? Without Müller and Beckenbauer on the one hand, Cruyff and Wim van Hanegem on the other, the 1974 finalists did not look well equipped.

Italy and France, two other leading European contenders, were aghast to be drawn in the same group as the host country. It proved to be a group in which the Hungarians, no minnows themselves,

could not even win a point. Indeed, the Argentinians only just beat Hungary (who had two men sent off) and the French, who went down to a dubious penalty which meant their elimination.

Brazil and West Germany were as unimpressive as each other in winning only one and drawing two of their group matches: yet Brazil still came close to reaching the final. Argentina had to win its last game against Peru 4–0 to pip Brazil – and amid much hysteria scored six.

Holland's match against Italy in the other second round

group became a semifinal; the winners went through. Dutch defender Ernie Brandts scored for each team before Arie Haan's magnificent 30-yard winner.

The final was rough, tough and dramatic. Mario Kempes, the only Argentinian exile brought back from Europe for the tournament, scored first only for Dirk Nanninga, a Dutch substitute, to equalize. Right on time Rob Rensenbrink's shot for Holland hit a post and in extra time it was Kempes again, scoring his sixth goal of the finals and making one for Daniel Bertoni.

Semifinals:
none (Brazil and Italy runners-up in second round groups)
Final:
Argentina 3 (Kempes 2, Bertoni)
Holland 1 (Nanninga)
(after extra time) 77,260

1982

Paolo Rossi, hero of the decisive stages of the 1982 matches in Spain, celebrates after scoring Italy's opening goal in the final against West Germany, who were outplayed in the second half.

Host: Spain
Winner: Italy

The biggest World Cup finals to date: 24 countries, 52 matches. Many people felt it was all too much. Standards around the world had undoubtedly levelled up and the closeness of groups in both rounds was a notable feature of the tournament.

Cameroon, drawn with Italy, Poland and Peru did not lose a match! Algeria beat West Germany and was only kept out of the next round by a quite deplorable non-aggression pact between the West Germans and Austrians.

Four more groups of three then had to be played. Poland, excelling again, won the first from the USSR. In the second England lost out to West Germany after goalless draws against them and a disappointing Spain. The third, played to packed houses in Barcelona, saw Italy beat the Argentinians, the holders, then devastate Brazil with a hat trick by Paolo Rossi, while the French, also improving with every game, easily won theirs.

So, at last, to the semifinals. Italy defeated Poland with two more goals by Rossi. France lost a 3–1 lead against the West Germans in a magnificent match marred only by goalkeeper Toni Schumacher's foul on Patrick Battiston and the unsatisfactory deciding penalty kicks which finished 5–4 in West Germany's favour.

The West Germans, though, played poorly in a final that gave the Italians three second-half goals and a third World Cup.

Semifinals:
Italy 2 Poland 0
West Germany 3 France 3 (after extra time: West Germany won on penalties)
Final:
Italy 3 (Rossi, Tardelli, Altobelli)
West Germany 1 (Breitner) 90,089

1986

The outstanding individual match of the 1986 finals was a quarter-final in Guadalajara between Brazil and France, which, sadly, had to be decided on penalties. Here the French midfielder Alain Giresse evades a challenge by Elzo.

**Host: Mexico
Winner: Argentina**

When Colombia decided in 1982 that it could not after all afford to stage the World Cup four years later, Brazil, Mexico, the United States and Canada were all keen to take over. With the Brazilian government refusing to back its association's bid, the way seemed clear for North America to host the tournament for the first time. To widespread astonishment, however, FIFA announced that only Mexico's application would be followed up, and duly awarded that country its second World Cup in 16 years.

A complex qualifying system involved several European nations in play-offs. Belgium defeated old rival Holland by the narrowest of margins; Scotland, having finished second to Spain, had to meet Australia, who posed unexpected problems before succumbing 0–2, 0–0. Only England of the European nations remained undefeated, winning four games and drawing four. Northern Ireland joined them in qualifying, to the exclusion of Romania. Wales missed out on goal difference; East Germany and Sweden by one point.

Paraguay won the play-off group against Peru, Chile and Colombia, which enabled them to join South America's big three: Brazil, Argentina and Uruguay.

Iraq and South Korea emerged as Asia's representatives; Algeria and Morocco came through the African section. With Canada winning the Central and North American group, there were five obvious minnows for the six groups in Mexico: Denmark, one of Europe's strongest teams, was absurdly nominated as the sixth. The teams seeded to head the groups, on the basis of past World Cup performances rather than current form, were Italy (holder), Mexico (host), France, Brazil, West Germany and Poland.

The Moroccans, who might have been expected to finish bottom of their group, provided the main surprise early on. Playing in the heat of Monterrey up in the north – the most tightly contested of the groups, it transpired – they held Poland and England to goalless draws before

1986

Gary Lineker's last England appearance as an Everton player was in the 2–1 defeat by Argentina. Immediately after the finals, having finished top scorer with six goals, he was transfered to Barcelona. Everton players Peter Reid (16) and Trevor Steven (17) offer typically close support.

defeating Portugal 3–1 to top the table.

The Portuguese, who had begun by beating England against the run of play, were thus condemned to bottom place while the English found some form and saved some face by defeating Poland 3–0 with a hat trick by Gary Lineker in the space of 26 minutes. They played that game without Ray Wilkins, sent off against Morocco, and Bryan Robson, who had dislocated his shoulder again. Since the 24 teams had to be reduced by only eight for the knockout stage, Poland still qualified, despite having finished third out of four.

The same thing applied in Group D, nicknamed *El Grupo de la Muerte* (the Group of Death) because

Denmark had been pitched in with West Germany, Uruguay (the South American champions) and Scotland.

It was the Scots who lost out, with odd-goal defeats by both Denmark and West Germany before a goalless draw against Uruguay, who held on after having Batista sent off in the very first minute.

Uruguay also had a player dismissed against the Danes, who went on to win 6–1, Elkjær scoring a hat trick. So Denmark qualified with maximum points, a feat matched only by Brazil in Group D, who went through with Spain.

Three teams qualified from Group B, where Mexico and Paraguay remained unbeaten and Belgium picked up three points. In Group

C France and the USSR both had five points, having drawn with each other, the Soviets' spectacular 6–1 demolition of Hungary giving them top place and an easier second round tie . . . or so it seemed.

The French found themselves pitted against the Italians, the holders, who had been held in their opening game by Bulgaria and consequently edged out of first position by Argentina. The French dominated the match and fully deserved their 2–0 win, earned by goals from Platini and Stopyra.

There were two surprises: Belgium overcame the USSR 4–3 in extra time despite a hat trick from Belanov; and then the Danes disintegrated against

Spain, who beat them 5–1 after trailing to Jesper Olsen's penalty. Emilio Butragueno scored four (having previously got a goal against Northern Ireland in 65 seconds, which won him a gold watch as the quickest of the tournament).

Pasculli's goal gave Argentina victory over Uruguay in a game that did not, as feared, become a brawl, and his side joined Brazil, Mexico, England and West Germany in the last eight.

The Germans put out Morocco in a poor game with Matthäus's 88th minute free kick. Brazil overcame Poland 4–0, though only after the unfortunate Poles had twice struck the woodwork and twice conceded a penalty. Mexico prompted more

1986

The third place match, in which France beat Belgium 4–2, was more entertaining than expected, given that both teams only wanted to go home and forget the disappointment of a semifinal defeat. Here Bernard Genghini, one of several reserves brought in by the French, loses out to Patrick Vervoort and Stéphane De Mol.

wild celebrations in the Azteca stadium, and later in the city centre, by defeating an unimaginative Bulgarian team with goals by Negrete – a superb volley – and Servin. And England followed up a 3–0 victory over Poland with another by the same score against Paraguay.

A knockout competition now became a penalty shoot-out: England's match against Argentina was the only quarter-final not to be decided on penalties. Surrounded by considerable ballyhoo in the wake of the Falklands War, it took on a new controversy when Diego Maradona clearly knocked the first goal past Shilton with his hand. Maradona then scored the most dazzling individual goal of the competition, but once Lineker pulled a goal back, the English could claim they deserved extra time at least.

France's tie against Brazil was a memorable one, too, for the quality of football and the drama of the penalty competition, in which Socrates and Platini both missed but Luis Fernandez converted the kick that took the

1986

Argentinian captain Diego Maradona, the tournament's outstanding figure, lifts the World Cup just a few minutes after supplying the pass for Jorge Burruchaga's winning goal.

French through.

West Germany gave a faultless display of penalty kicks to oust Mexico after a goalless draw, and the Belgians produced another surprise, somewhat luckily holding Spain 1–1 before putting their penalties away more effectively.

They found Maradona as unstoppable as England had; two more outstanding individual goals from him took Argentina through to the final, where their opponents would be not France, as most neutrals had hoped, but West Germany. The Germans capitalised on goalkeeper Joel Bats's first error of the tournament, when he allowed Brehme's free kick to slide under him, and Völler added a second with almost the last kick.

It was the West Germans' fifth final in nine tournaments and, having come from behind to win twice previously, in 1954 and 1974, they were perhaps less dismayed than England and Belgium had been to go two down to the Argentinians through Brown and Valdano. In a dramatic last 15 minutes two left-wing corners brought goals for Rummenigge and Völler. But Maradona was not prepared to see his dream destroyed: within three minutes he had sent Burruchaga through to join the ranks of those whose goals have won the World Cup.

Semifinals:
Argentina 2 Belgium 0
West Germany 2
France 0
Final: Argentina 3
(Brown, Valdano,
Burruchaga)
West Germany 2
(Rummenigge, Völler)
114,580

INDEX

ACKNOWLEDGEMENTS

The publishers thank the following for providing the photographs in this book:

All Sport (David Cannon) 4, 34, 38, 44, 54 above right, 55 below right, 56 above left and below right, 62, 76; (Trevor Jones) 9; (Michael King) 59 above; (Mike Powell) 54 below left, (Steve Powell) 55 above right; (Billy Stickland) 77, 78, 79; Associated Press 32, 51, above left, 58 below; Colorsport 6, 8, 10, 11, 12, 13, 14, 17, 19, 20, 21, 22, 25, 26, 29, 33, 40, 41, 49, 50 above left, right and below left, 52 below left and right, 53 top left, below right and mid left; 54 mid left, below right and above left; 55 above, mid and below left, 56 mid right and below left, 57, 59 below, 60, 64; Photo Source 16, 51 below left, 52 above left, 53 mid right and below left, 66 above and below, 67 above, 68, 69, 70; Presse Sports 43, 47; Rex/SIPA Press 52 mid left; Sporting Pictures 24, 27; Syndication International 7, 30, 31, 36, 37, 46, 50 mid and below right, 51 above and below right, mid left, 52 above right, 71, 72, 73, 74; Bob Thomas Sports Photography 2, 15, 18, 23, 28, 35, 39, 42, 48, 56 above right, 61, 65, 75, 79; Topham 67 below.